VICTORIES NEVER LAST

VICTORIES NEVER LAST

...

Reading and Caregiving in a Time of Plague

ROBERT ZARETSKY

The University of Chicago Press
CHICAGO AND LONDON

The University of Chicago Press, Chicago 60637
The University of Chicago Press, Ltd., London

Published 2022
Printed in the United States of America

31 30 29 28 27 26 25 24 23 22   1 2 3 4 5

ISBN-13: 978-0-226-80349-4 (cloth)
ISBN-13: 978-0-226-80352-4 (e-book)
DOI: https://doi.org/10.7208/chicago/9780226803524.001.0001

Library of Congress Cataloging-in-Publication Data

Names: Zaretsky, Robert, 1955– author.
Title: Victories never last : reading and caregiving in a time of plague / Robert Zaretsky.
Description: Chicago : University of Chicago Press, 2022. | Includes index.
Identifiers: LCCN 2021037125 | ISBN 9780226803494 (cloth) | ISBN 9780226803524 (e-book)
Subjects: LCSH: Plague in literature. | Epidemics in literature. | European literature—History and criticism. | COVID-19 Pandemic, 2020– —Social aspects.
Classification: LCC PN56.P5 Z37 2022 | DDC 809/.933561—dc23/eng/20211118
LC record available at https://lccn.loc.gov/2021037125

♾ This paper meets the requirements of ANSI/NISO Z39.48-1992 (Permanence of Paper).

"I've never managed to get used to seeing people die."
"But your victories will never be lasting; that's all."

Exchange between Dr. Bernard Rieux and Jean Tarrou

ALBERT CAMUS, *THE PLAGUE*

CONTENTS

VICTORIES NEVER LAST

INTRODUCTION

> Plagues are a feature of the human experience. What happened in 2020 was not new to our species. It was just new to us.
>
> NICHOLAS CHRISTAKIS

> Pitted against microbial genes, we have mainly our wits.
>
> JOSHUA LEDERBURG

For more than forty years as a reader and writer, student and teacher, I have thought that literature and life are deeply bound to one another. This, at least, has been the case for me. The novels I read and events I live merge into one another—a tidal motion of sorts that, I believe, has enriched my imagination and enlarged my sensibility. The sort of attention that literature asks of us while we read has the happy knack of carrying over into the lives we lead.

In early March 2020, when the novel coronavirus exploded into our lives, I thus turned to the more familiar kind of novel in order to put the pieces back to my own life. Too predictably, perhaps, they were novels—as well as essays and histories—that all deal, in one way or another, with the reality of plagues and our individual and communal, political and philosophical responses to them. I did so with neither a plan nor a project in mind, simply turning at first to writers whose voices were familiar and whose writings have long kept me company: Thucydides and Marcus Aurelius, Michel de Montaigne and Albert Camus. I have written a good deal on Camus over the years and in a variety of courses have taught Thucydides, Marcus Aurelius, and Montaigne.

All of these writers had known plagues firsthand. A survivor of the great plague that swept through Athens in 430–429 BCE, Thucydides described it in his *History of the Peloponnesian War*. Marcus Aurelius was Rome's emperor during the Antonine Plague that raged from 165 to 180 CE. Though Marcus Aurelius only briefly refers to it in his *Meditations*, the plague had a significant impact on his worldview. As for Montaigne, the inventor of the essay form was also the mayor of Bordeaux when, in 1585, it was battered by a great wave of bubonic plague. He wrote his last and most gripping essays, including "On Experience," as a survivor of plague. Though Camus never faced a bacteriological plague, he battled a life-threatening ideological plague during the German occupation of France. His decision to distill this experience into the metaphor of plague, while criticized in his own lifetime, now seems all too apt in our own age of bacteriological and ideological plagues.

This time, though, their voices sounded different. This was unsurprising: quite suddenly, my life and world had also become different. My long life has been a fortunate one, free of the kinds of existential crises to which I have nevertheless devoted much of my writing and reading. It was a life, in short, free of most pestilences. For the first time, I was reading these works in a time of plague. Voices that were once familiar and comforting now struck me as edgy and tinged with urgency. It was as if the bright red chyrons unspooling along the bottom of flat screens had breached the books I was reading.

Those chyrons threaded their way across the pages of other books I now began to read for the first time. While writing *The Plague*, Camus had turned for guidance not only to Thucydides and Montaigne, but also to Daniel Defoe. The epigram that begins the novel happens to come from *Robinson Crusoe*. But it was the French translation of another Defoe novel, *A Journal of the Plague Year*, that Camus mined for insights while living under and resisting *la peste brune*, or the "brown plague" of the Nazi occupation. While the worldviews of the narrators in the two novels differ greatly, the logic of the narratives not just resemble one another, but also suggest ways in which to make sense of our current plague.

Camus was not alone to look to Defoe for insight; so, too, did Mary Shelley. Though I had read and taught *Frankenstein; Or, the Modern Prometheus*, I somehow never knew that she had written another novel steeped in death and dread, *The Last Man*. That book was published a half-dozen years after *Frankenstein*—years of great financial and emotional distress during which she had lost her husband Percy Bysshe Shelley and two of their three children—and was an utter flop. Blasted by the critics (all of whom happened to be men) and ignored by the public, the novel disappeared from the European literary landscape for nearly two centuries. Yet I found that in our own transformed microbiological and ideological landscape, Shelley's voice sounds so very sharp and clear.

When my university shuttered the campus and shifted online halfway through the semester, I became a teacher without a classroom and sought, with questionable success, to find my footing in Zoomscape. Soon after, I found myself in yet another unfamiliar world. At the suggestion of a dear and distressed friend, I began volunteer work at her nearby nursing home. The residence, which had entered lockdown, was understaffed and overwhelmed by the unprecedented situation. Keen to help in whatever way I could, I was tested and cleared to work as a hospitality aide. Every day between 3:30 and 6:30 p.m., my job was to deliver dinner trays to the nearly 100 residents who, with the dining room now darkened, took their meals in their rooms. As a third or so of the residents, most of whom were suffering from dementia, were unable to feed themselves, my task was also to help them eat their meals.

My days as a hospitality aide grew into weeks, and my weeks into months. My circumstances at the residence were not by any stretch of any imagination like those confronting first responders in our emergency rooms. Even less did my experiences resemble the unspeakable tragedies unfolding in those nursing homes long subject to neglect. During the nearly three months I worked at the residence, thanks largely to its determined staff, there was not a single case of COVID-19—a relatively remarkable feat in Texas.

But this success came at great human cost. Isolation from their families and fellow residents chipped away at the minds of most residents. Though the tireless activities director worked hard at maintaining the morale of the residents—blaring Frank Sinatra over boom boxes and emceeing bingo games with the residents playing from their rooms—loneliness and confusion nevertheless became the default conditions of residential life. Three residents on hospice at whose bedsides I spent long afternoons died from causes other than COVID-19. Their deaths were not a surprise, but they were nevertheless shocking: in effect, they died alone. The deterioration of others on hospice before the lockdown seemed to quicken, as if I was watching a time-lapse film whose speed slowly accelerated. The neuroscientist John Cacioppo's estimate that chronic loneliness increases the odds of an early death by 20 percent suddenly seemed too conservative.[1]

At the same time, spiraling demands on the staff widened the social and ethnic fissures at the residence. The CNAs (certified nursing aides) with whom I worked were almost entirely Hispanic and African American. They moved the residents from their beds to wheelchairs, wheelchairs to toilets and showers, and back to their beds, all the while chatting and pattering. They bagged soiled sheets and undergarments, but they earned the same hourly wage as McDonald's workers who bagged burgers and fries. While the nurses, who were mostly white, measured the vital signs of the residents, the CNAs mostly attended to other, but equally vital signs that instruments cannot measure.

The virus seemed to be everywhere and nowhere. On the one hand, the residence was COVID-19 free. Moreover, unlike other pestilential diseases like smallpox, cholera, and bubonic plague, this virus did not manifest itself in visible and violent ways. On the other hand, though, the disease's presence, like the ashen clouds over the nearby oil refineries, settled on the nursing home. It was the only subject of the cable and local news channels, usually playing at full volume—and often tuned to different stations—over the two flat screens bolted to the walls in each of the rooms. It was the ostensible subject of the daily press briefings from the White House, whose real subject was almost always the press briefing's master of ceremonies. It was the usual subject of conversation among staff workers frazzled by the shortage of masks and gowns and puzzled by the muddle of messages from national and local leaders.

The tragic consequences of isolation and loneliness were compounded in October—a few months after I had to stop my regular hours at the nursing home, but still helped there from time to time—when the state's governor, Greg Abbott, ordered that nursing homes again allow visitations. Though the order was welcomed by the residents' families, it was dreaded by the staff. Already scrambling to do the bare minimum, they had neither the means nor the manpower to oversee the visits. With a kind of awful inevitability, the virus breached the walls of the residence and, by year's end, took the lives of more than a dozen residents, many of whom I had joked with and offered spoonsful of tapioca just a few months earlier. We were not unique—by the end of 2020, 40 percent of COVID-related deaths in the United States occurred at nursing homes—but that did not lessen the shock or shame. As the physician and sociologist Nicholas Christakis recently observed, nursing homes became the inadvertent twenty-first-century equivalent of the "pesthouses" that sheltered long-ago plague sufferers.[2]

What to do about this uninvited and uncanny guest in our world? How should we respond to it? Jean Tarrou, a character in *The Plague*, makes the case for attention. "We must keep endless watch on ourselves lest in a careless moment we breathe in somebody's face and fasten the microbe on him," he insists. "What's natural is the microbe. All the rest—health, integrity, purity (if you like)—is a product of human will, a vigilance that must never falter." Without such attention, Tarrou believed, nothing good and lasting can be achieved. In their various ways, all of these writers practice attention.

With the exception of Marcus Aurelius, who wrote reminders and remonstrations to himself concerning his thoughts and acts, these writers turned to narrative in order to exercise their attention. Instead of offering arguments, they offer stories; rather than affirming truth-claims of one sort or another, they affirm what Iris Murdoch famously called the "density of our lives." If literature can be said to have a task, she concluded, "that surely is its task."[3] I believe the stories told by these earlier writers help us touch the density of this pandemic and its impact on the world and ourselves. For this same reason, while I turn to these texts to help direct my attention toward the context of my life and the contexts of other lives, I have also written stories of my own experiences at the nursing home. Though no Tarrou, I have tried to be as vigilant as possible about others and myself; though no Murdoch, I have tried my hand at philosophy and literature in order to make sense of life's density. My reading and working experiences are, to echo Montaigne, "the matter of this book." These writers have helped me better see the world, perhaps even myself. They might encourage other readers to turn to them in the expectation that they will do the same.

1

THUCYDIDES AND THE GREAT PLAGUE OF ATHENS

Thucydides as the grand summation, the last manifestation of that strong, stern, hard matter-of-factness instinctive to the older Hellenes. FRIEDRICH NIETZSCHE

Indeed, this was the greatest movement yet known in history, not only of the Hellenes, but the large part of the barbarian world—I had almost said of mankind. THUCYDIDES

Down Apollo strode from Olympus' peaks, storming at his
heart
with his bow and hooded quiver slung across his shoulders.
The arrows clanged at his back as the god quaked with rage,
the god himself on the march and down he came like night.
Over against the ships he dropped to a knee, let fly a shaft
and a terrifying clash rang out from the great silver bow.
First he went for the mules and circling dogs but then,
launching a piercing shaft at the men themselves,
he cut them down in droves—and the corpse-fires burned on,
night and day, no end in sight.

Famously, Homer opens the *Iliad* with his plea to the muse to explain the wrath of the demigod Achilles. Less famously, the poet then pivots to the rage of the god Apollo. We learn that, responding to the prayer of his priest Chryses, whose daughter Chryseis had been taken by Agamemnon as a war prize, Apollo launches a deadly plague against the Achaean king's army. The pestilential storm continues nine days until Achilles intervenes, demanding that Agamemnon surrender Chryseis. The king agrees on one condition—that Achilles hand over his own war prize, Briseis. Enraged, Achilles accepts the deal, quits the invasion, and storms off with his companion Patroclus. The insult-strewn confrontation between the two Achaeans leads eventually not just to their own deaths, but also to the destruction of Troy and the decimation of the Achaeans.

Western literature thus begins not with ire but, as the classicist Mary Beard observed, with infection.[1] Infection, in turn, begins not with men, but with the gods. The bards of Archaic Greece, including Homer, knew the source of such plagues. Such events are all in a day's work for the denizens of Olympus. Among Apollo's many epithets is Smintheus, which may well mean "mouse-god." Not an especially terrifying epithet, granted, until you recall the close family ties between mice and rats. So close, in fact, that the ancient Greeks used the two names interchangeably.[2] Indeed, it is conceivable that these same rats from eastern Troy accompanied the Achaeans on their ships as they made their way westward and back home to Greece.

In any case, it is hardly accidental that Chryses calls Apollo by this name in his pained appeal on his daughter's behalf. Nor is it accidental that Homer chooses to begin his epic with the tableau not of men falling in battle, but instead falling from plague. After all, the Achaean invaders had spent nine years in what was meant to be a temporary base outside the walls of Troy. It is not the muse's job to delve into details, but readers can easily imagine the camp's ramshackle state of sanitation and hygiene. No wonder that there is no mention of pestilence inside Troy.

A city adorned with "magnificent palaces" like Priam's and cold streams where women washed "their glistening robes" no doubt had the means to have safer ways of disposing of human waste and human bodies. The beached and becalmed Achaeans, viewing the city from their camp, must have yearned for more than its riches. They also yearned for a bath.

Moreover, if the plague did travel from east to west, it makes historical sense to launch the story about the collision between "eastern" Troy and "western" Greece with an account of plague. The establishment of farming communities in the Middle East, which became more prone to disease as they grew larger and denser, exported microbes as well as other materials to the west with the expansion of commercial travel across the Mediterranean. The Aegean gateway, William McNeill observes in his landmark study *Plagues and Peoples*, became an ideal path for both macro-parasitism and micro-parasitism. Plague was the cost of people doing business.

No less important, it makes ethical sense for Homer to begin with pestilence. As the poem will reveal in unflinching detail, the costs and consequences of the war are as great as those of the plague. It is as if the plague allows Homer to depict, in distilled form, what has already happened outside Troy's walls and will happen inside those same walls. Warriors will fall and pyres will burn; trauma will accompany those who survive, trauma that leads to greater rage and more massacres. The plague turns Achilles's world upside down, ransacking his value system. His concern for his fellow Achaeans, leading him to confront Agamemnon, leads to his moral undoing. Shorn of the earned honor embodied by Briseis, Achilles proves that his wrath is as great as Apollo's.

...

Thucydides had a complicated relationship with Homer. Both of them understood that, while we may not be interested in war,

war is interested in us. One of the reasons Thucydides chose to write on the war between Athens and Sparta—as was also true of his immediate predecessor Herodotus's account of the Persian Wars—was, no doubt, because Homer had written on war. No other topic, he believed, was a better test of *kleos*, or renown, and thus worthier of a heroic narrative. Besides, as Homer's epic was the measure of literary greatness, what choice did subsequent writers have but to take up the challenge? In effect, Thucydides labored under the anxiety of influence. He could not live with Homer yet could not live without him. Confronting the poet's challenge, Thucydides chose to write on war as well. Yet his account would prove more lasting than Homer's because he would base it on a war of greater moment. If the Trojan War was, from a poetic perspective, the war to begin all wars, the Peloponnesian War would be, from a philosophical perspective, the war to end all interpretations of war.

This explains the claim, bordering on hubris, Thucydides makes at the very opening of his history. He undertook this *historia*, or inquiry, because he believed "that it would be a great war, and more worthy of relation than any that had preceded it." Making clear that this was not a slip of the stylus, he adds a few sentences later: "Indeed, this was the greatest movement yet known in history, not only of the Hellenes, but the large part of the barbarian world—I had almost said of mankind" (1.1). Paradoxically, *stasis* is the Greek word for movement or convulsion. By stasis, Thucydides means the state of tension created by opposing forces, each of which seek to dominate the other. Such tension exists both within groups—for example, the confrontation between Achilles and Agamemnon—but also between groups like the Greeks and Trojans. Thucydides applies the word to the eventual and inevitable confrontation between Athens and Sparta. Allies in their struggle against the Persians fifty years earlier, the city-states had now become antagonists.

By virtue of their respective virtues—one was an expanding sea power, the other a retiring land power; one was an open society that cultivated the intellectual arts, the other a closed society that cultivated the martial arts—Athens and Sparta were bound for gory collision.

For Thucydides, the uses of stasis do not stop there. A related kind of stasis—statistics—is the means by which he will show that this collision was greater than the Trojan War. By averaging out the number of warriors who, according to Homer, sailed with two different fleets to Troy, he concludes that the actual number of men was not nearly as great as the poet implies. Certainly not as considerable, in any case, as those mobilized during the Peloponnesian War—even if, as Thucydides maliciously adds, he accepts Homer's numbers at face value, despite the "exaggeration which a poet would feel himself licensed to employ" (1.11). Thucydides bests this burn, thus scoring the stasis between him and Homer, a few paragraphs later when he warns his readers that there is "an absence of romance" in his history. He has not written, after all, "to win the applause of the moment, but as a possession for all time" (1.23). Roll over, Calliope, Clio is here. The muse of epic poetry must give way to the muse of history. In this most personal instance of stasis, Thucydides challenges Homer. The burning darts of Apollo that assail the Achaeans will thus be replaced by the burning pustules that afflict the Athenians.

...

The reason his work was timeless, Thucydides explained, is because in "the course of human things" the future resembles the past. As a result, he clearly believed we can anticipate the various outcomes of a given situation. Whether Thucydides also believed that our ability to anticipate the course of events is matched by our ability to correct, when necessary, that same course is less clear. Take the nursing home: the place is steeped in stasis. The historian need look no further than a typical room, each of which boasts a flat screen for each of the two residents. They are almost always on and, since most of the residents are hard of hearing, they are almost always blasting. Sometimes the effect is stereophonic because the sets are tuned to the same channel; sometimes the effect is cacophonic because they are fixed on different stations; at almost all times, the effect is jarring.

Occasionally, the residents clash over their choice of stations. The confrontations are Homeric only if you imagine Priam and Phoenix arguing over the respective merits of javelins and swords. One afternoon, as I passed the room of Mrs. J and Mrs. F, the former pivoted her wheelchair in my direction. Wide-girthed and gray-haired, her face mask draped around her neck like a scarf, she glowered at me. "Could you please help lower the volume on Mrs. F's television?" she shouted. I looked over at Mrs. F, a small woman who skips between lucidity and fantasy with elfin grace. She was sitting in her custom lounge chair, watching Wolf Blitzer on CNN. Assuming that neither woman could figure out how to use the remote, I walked over to her bed, picked up the remote control, and lowered the volume several clicks. As I did so, the voice of Bret Baier, the Fox News anchor who was staring down at me from Mrs. J's screen, filled whatever space had been left by Blitzer. As it dawned on me that I had become, like an Achaean or Trojan soldier, a pawn in a much larger battle, Mrs. F sharply announced: "That's *my* television. My family bought it for me." Setting the remote back on the bed and stepping toward the door, I looked at the two roommates. "The two of you will need to agree on the volumes you can both live with. You can find a compromise, right?" Without waiting for an answer, I slipped out the door and down the hallway.

Was the dispute over national politics? Or was it instead over local power? Over who should call the shots in our country, or who should call the shots in their room? I didn't know and I don't think Mrs. J and Mrs. F knew either. It was as if the verbal static cascading from the screens into their small room—piled high with framed photos of their families, personalized throw pillows, and wilting flowers from Mother's Day—ignited the stasis that had been building since the lockdown. Compounding the pathos, it is not clear they understand the differences between the discourses on their screens any better than the diagnoses of their doctors. In any event, since that skirmish, the two women seem to have struck a truce. Or, more accurately, struck a reef. Preoccupied by their shared predicament, the roommates have muted the static and are waiting for the storm to pass.

...

"The extent and mortality of the pestilence—said to have begun somewhere in the east—was nowhere remembered. Neither were the physicians at first of any service, ignorant as they were of the proper way to treat it. Various methods were tried, but they proved futile: the disease overwhelmed all of them." Thucydides thus begins his account of the plague that strikes Athens in 430 BCE. He had read not only Homer, but Hippocrates. Like the founder of Western medicine, who emphasized the importance of describing the evolution of a disease, so too with the founder of Western history. "I shall simply set down," Thucydides declares, "the nature of this disease and explain the symptoms by which perhaps it may be recognized by the student if it should ever break out again." He then proceeds to depict in vivid detail the plague's impact on individuals. "From one moment to the next, healthy people were stricken by violent headaches and inflamed eyes. Their breath turning fetid, they were wracked by sneezing and coughing fits; their skin blistering with pustules, they threw off their clothing and threw themselves into water tanks in their frenzied quest for relief. Spasms of diarrhea, weakening what remained of the body's resistance, signaled the imminence of death." Racked by other internal disorders, the afflicted suffered as long as a week before dying.

Indeed, it proved impossible to fend off death. "No remedy was found that could be used as a specific; for what did good in one case, did harm in another. Strong and weak constitutions proved equally incapable of resistance, all alike being swept away." The unprecedented force of the disease overwhelmed not just the body, but the mind. Baffled by the seemingly random character of the plague, which carried off rich and poor, healthy and sick, free men and slaves, Athenians fell into despondency. Yet gloom was a sure invitation to death, Thucydides remarks, for it "instantly took away their power of resistance and left them a much easier prey to the disorder" (2.51).

Describing the disease was as difficult as defending against it. "The nature of the distemper was such," Thucydides observes, "as to baffle all description and its attacks almost too grievous for human nature to endure" (2.50). This claim was based on personal experience: not only did Thucydides witness the progression of the disease among his fellow Athenians but, as he tells us, he had himself been stricken by it. Having survived to describe his symptoms, he is not interested in identifying the disease's nature, leaving that task to "other writers, whether lay or professional," the task of identifying it. Over the past century or so, other writers—both classicists and epidemiologists—have taken up the challenge. Candidates have ranged from smallpox and scarlet fever to bubonic plague and Ebola; none of them, though, neatly fits the description left by Thucydides. (The recent discovery of an ancient mass burial site in Athens—stumbled across by workers tunneling into the ground for a new subway station—might settle the debate. Taking DNA samples from the old bones, researchers found traces of *salmonella enterica serovar Typhi*, the pathogen for typhus.[3])

Instead, Thucydides moves from the disease's impact on the human body to its impact on the body politic. Stumped by the disease's unprecedented nature, the physicians died more rapidly than those they tried to cure. Others who, compelled by honor and loyalty, tended to the ill also fell victims to the plague. As for those who instead ignored such duties and isolated themselves at home, they also died, but alone and forlorn. More disturbingly, just as the "mortality raged without restraint," men too began to rage without restraint. Temples became morgues, "full of corpses of persons that had died there, just as they were," while funeral pyres became free-for-alls, with panicked mourners fighting over access to the fires or simply tossing bodies on top of flames lit by other families.

Worse was to come, as traditional rites turned into near riots as the still living—or, rather, the not yet dead—"became utterly careless of everything, whether sacred or profane" (2.52). With the caving of rituals came the cratering of order, with men "now coolly venturing on what they had formerly done in a corner." As "fear of gods or law of man" decayed and disappeared, misrule became the rule. The virtue by which Achilles lived and died—honor—was now "popular with none," since there was no prospect of living long enough to enjoy its rewards. As a result, immediate gratification was newly considered "honorable and useful." Under the shadow of death, Athenians regarded "their lives and riches as alike things of a day." As for those without riches but still with their lives, we are left to imagine their actions, since Thucydides—the offspring of an old and aristocratic family—does not bother to say.

...

With the eclipse of the "fear of gods or law of man," the city's *nomoi* withered and died. The Greek word means laws, but also something more fundamental: the conventions, conduct, and customs of a society. *Nomoi* is what Americans call norms; war and disease reveal, then as now, how fragile they are. And how fragile they were, say, in seventeenth-century England. In 1628—the same year that King Charles I dissolved the Parliament, a pivotal step toward the civil wars that would explode little more than a decade later—an English translation of Thucydides's history appeared. It was the first to be based on the original Greek text and the translator, who had published little else, explained his reason for taking on the thick and dense work. It is, he explained, the principal and proper work of history "to instruct and enable men, by the knowledge of actions past, to bear themselves prudently in the present and providently towards the future: there is not extant any other (merely human) that doth more naturally and fully perform it, than this of my author."

Did Thomas Hobbes, the translator who would leap from obscurity to notoriety in 1651 with the publication of *Leviathan*, turn to Thucydides as he reflected on the course of the civil wars? Scholars seem certain he had, with one going so far as to conclude that Hobbes's ideas about human behavior "read like generalizations from Thucydides' examples."[4] The more interesting question, perhaps, is what Thucydides, if he could time-travel, would have made of Hobbes. A sign, indeed, that his work was a possession for all time. More a pathologist of social than biological events, Thucydides is less the follower of Hippocrates than he is the forerunner to Hobbes. Like the Englishman, Thucydides is most concerned by the dire social ramifications set in motion by the disease's ravages. Indeed, Athens seemed to dissolve into a Hobbesian state of nature, that "dissolute condition of masterless men, without subjection to laws, reduced to continual fear and danger of violent death; and life of man solitary, brutish, nasty and short." And Thucydides would no doubt find in Hobbes someone who has no more need of the gods or god to make sense of events than he did.

...

Signs of faith, predictably, ran riot in many of the rooms where I delivered the food trays. There were crosses on the walls, Bibles on the beds, statues of Jesus Christ on the night tables. Sundays brought both quiet and disquiet. As the residents could not leave and priests or ministers could not enter the building, all parties were reduced to televised broadcasts. Despite living in the age of televangelism, the residents seemed distracted and detached from the sermons and ceremonies. They were like children placed in isolation, asked to make do with a televised image of a burning Yule log for Christmas, with neither warmth nor odor from a real fire or a real family. The stations of the cross were replaced by the stations on the screen; the medium, not their man in Bethlehem, had become the message.

Yet other rooms, including a few whose residents were on hospice care, were bare of religious signage. I walked quietly past these rooms, whether out of respect or cowardice, I cannot say. Still other rooms were bare of religious mementos, but full of life. This, at least, was the case for the home's Gloria Swanson, Mrs. A. Her darkened half of the room—divided by a solid partition rather than a curtain—smacked of Sunset Boulevard, ornate and thick with family memorabilia and fashion magazines. Always propped up in her bed as if waiting for a curtain to rise, Mrs. A presided over her small world. Graced with wild gray hair, teardrop eyeglasses, and a spotted leopard coat, she was surrounded by snack bags, crosswords, and books.

Mrs. A smiled widely at me, then turned her attention back to her television. Looking at the screen, I saw Paul Henried, an actor whose smoldering gaze and aristocratic bearing graced movie theaters in the 1940s. I wish I could report the movie was *Now, Voyager*, but the female lead, whoever she was, was not Bette Davis.

But I can report that one of the books on Mrs. A's bed was that Bible for Texas progressives, Molly Ivins's *Bushwhacked*. Ivins made great sport of skewering Texas politicians who mixed Christian faith with public policy, warning that if God kept hanging out with them, it would hurt his reputation. She was especially ruthless with George W. Bush and, until her death in 2007, lambasted his fatal mixture of machismo posturing and Christian convictions that had led our country to Iraq.

"Gads, I miss her!" I blurted to Mrs. A. Still staring at the screen, Mrs. A replied, "So do I!" I was about to share Ivins's quip about Texas Baptists—"They are not kept under water long enough"—but then realized Mrs. A thought I meant the glamorous woman on the screen. "I meant Molly," I explained, while gesturing to the book. Mrs. A looked confusedly at the cover, then at me. She no more knew who Molly Ivins, I suddenly grasped, than I knew who the actress was. Looking back at the screen, I announced, "Gads, I miss Hollywood!" Mrs. A relaxed and smiled again. A few minutes later, and I left the room thinking I was the one who needed a good dunking.

...

Ancient spirits are nowhere to be found in Thucydides's explanation of the causes to the series of seismic events, including the plague, he recounts in his history. Whether he believed in the gods, we will probably never know. What we do know, however, is that he makes no room for the gods and goddesses in his historical account. Like the French scientist Pierre Laplace who, when asked by Napoleon why he made no mention of God in his books, replied, "I have no need for that hypothesis," Thucydides had no need for those higher beings. At best, the denizens of Olympus might well be watching events below, but they have no more control or concern over what they see than do the denizens at the nursing home over what they see on their screens. Though the antagonists in the history refer and defer to what they take to be auguries, the gods and goddesses are missing in action in Thucydides's analysis of events. It is a world in which, as one classicist recently concluded, "humans confront an impersonal and almost Newtonian system of behavior."[5]

This explains, in part, his indifference to the question of the plague's origins. When he writes that he will leave this matter to others, whether lay or professional, Thucydides no doubt includes the priests. He drily notes that the usual religious rites at the start of the plague went unanswered. "Supplications in the temples, divinations, and so forth were found equally futile, till the overwhelming nature of the disaster at last put a stop to them altogether" (2.47). Existentialism was not among the schools of philosophy founded in ancient Greece, yet the historian's depiction of the disconnect between the desperate entreaties made by priests and the stubborn silence of the gods will strike modern readers as deeply absurd.

Many fellow Athenians no doubt despaired over this silence, but Thucydides did not. Hence the countless ascriptions to him as the father of objective or scientific history. The admiring Friedrich Nietzsche takes the praise a step further, declaring that this austere and severe Greek had no need for any recourse to the transcendental. In *Twilight of the Idols,* he declares that reading Thucydides offers him, more so than any other ancient writer, "recreation, preference and cure from all Platonism."

For the German thinker, it boils down to a matter of clarity and courage. “Courage in the face of reality ultimately distinguishes such natures as Thucydides and Plato: Plato is a coward in the face of reality—consequently he flees into the ideal; Thucydides has *himself* under control—consequently he retains control over things.”[6]

Of course, the claims made by political theorists for Thucydides's austere objectivity—not to mention Nietzsche's claim for his Übermensch-like courage—must be taken with a grain of salt. Or, for a new generation of classicists, more than a few grains. As Robert Connor has observed, objectivity in the *History* is not an end, but a means; not a goal, but a strategy. By casting himself as an objective observer, Thucydides established a relationship “between reader and author, not one between author and his subject matter.”[7] But even as an authorial stance, and not an authentic sentiment, Thucydides's refusal to countenance any divine role in the causes and consequences of the plague forces us to reflect. In Connor's beautiful phrase, Thucydides's history “does not teach us how to control human events, nor enable us to cure plagues or prevent potential tyrannies, but it reminds us how easily men can move from the illusion of control over events to being controlled by them—from action to pathos.”[8] In a word, we move from history to tragedy.

...

Outside the *History*, the account of the plague is terrifying; within the *History*, it is terrifying and tragic. In Thucydides's organization of the material, the plague blasts Athens a few scarce sentences after Pericles, the city's great *strategos* or general, praises the city. His funeral oration—largely the invention of Thucydides—is the *History*'s most celebrated passage. It became, Garry Wills remarks, “the most famous oration of its kind, a model endlessly copied, praised and cited."[9] The most important instance of its influence, Wills continues, was Abraham Lincoln's address at Gettysburg. Both orations are given to extol those who had fallen for the nation, but more importantly to explain the reasons for their sacrifice. Pericles and Lincoln come not just to bury their fellow countrymen, but to praise them.

In both orations, however, the praise subtly shifts from the dead soldiers to the living ideals of the young nations. For Pericles, these ideals are reflected in his city's *nomoi*. In the first instance, *nomos* means nothing more than "law." On this score, Pericles makes clear that Athens always leads, never follows. "Our constitution does not copy the laws of neighboring states; we are rather a pattern to others than imitators ourselves." In a sharp poke at his conservative critics, Pericles affirms that this young democracy insists that the laws apply equally to all men, as must the opportunity for advancement regardless of one's social or economic status. The laws and institutions of Athens, in short, "favor the many instead of the few; this is why it is called a democracy" (2.37).

But again, *nomos* is also something more than mere law. It points to something deeper, something foundational, something that marks the shift from laws to norms. Athens's practices and traditions are no less essential to its identity than its architecture and army. As with its temples and phalanxes, so too with its ethics: measure and balance inform them all. Pericles portrays an Athens that is daring, but never rash; open, but always vigilant; selfless, yet moved by enlightened self-interest. It allows its citizens to pursue their private ends, but also expects them to prepare for public duties. "We regard the citizen who takes no part in these duties not as unambitious but as useless" (2.40). Such is the Athens, Pericles announces, for which these men fought and died. Such is the Athens, he affirms, that is an "education for all of Greece" (2.41).

So, too, is this the Athens that offers an education on the fragility of those same *nomoi*. Thucydides arranges his material so that the moment Pericles concludes his oration, the plague begins. This unknown unknown upends the strategy that, Pericles insisted, would eventually carry the day against the Spartans. Key to that strategy was the use of walls and ships. With the approach of the feared Spartan soldiers, the agrarian families in the surrounding region of Attica would retreat behind the long walls connecting the harbor and city whose construction Pericles had overseen. At the same time, the equally fearsome Athenian fleets would be making life miserable for Sparta and its allies. Let us not worry, Pericles urged in a speech before the war, about our fields and houses. Unlike Sparta, chained to the land, Athens was master of the sea. Let us then imagine Athens as an island, he suggested, for it was effectively true: "The rule of the sea is indeed a great matter" (1.143).

Yet merchant and military ships carry not just material and men, but also vermin and viruses. Compounding this irony was that the transfer of the rural population to the city, squeezing them behind walls already bulging with 300,000 or so inhabitants, was meant to ensure their safety. All of the necessary ingredients for an epidemic were thus joined, waiting for a chance event or encounter to set it aflame. As the Spartans destroy the fields outside the walls and the pestilence decimates the people within the walls, Pericles finds himself assailed by the same assembly that had previously applauded him. Refusing to concede that he made mistakes, he describes the plague as "sudden, unexpected and least within calculation" (2.61). Yet the Athenian assembly, overcome by panic and anger, nevertheless fines Pericles and removes him from his post. Mirroring the flux of events, the assembly soon has second thoughts and re-elects Pericles as general. Shortly after, however, the one man whose integrity and ability made him capable of "leading the Athenians rather than being led" (2.65) also falls victim to the plague—a last ironic turn worthy of the tragic playwrights.

...

Sophocles, for one, could have scripted that moment. In fact, sometime during the decade following the plague, he *did* script this moment. His play *Oedipus the King* may well have been performed in 426 BCE, the moment that the second (and not first) wave of the plague began to subside. An audience of stunned survivors thus witnessed Oedipus's tragic decision to battle the plague ravaging his native Thebes—tragic because, done with the best of intentions, the decision undoes Oedipus and, eventually, Thebes itself.

At the play's opening, Thebes is foundering "beneath a weltering surge of blood." A blight, the Chorus announces, "is on our harvest in the ear / A blight upon the grazing flocks and herds / A blight on wives in travail; and withal / Armed with his blazing torch the God of Plague / Hath swooped upon our city emptying the house of Cadmus / And the murky realm of Pluto is full fed with groans and tears." The cries of anguish reach King Oedipus, who is already hailed by Thebans for his wisdom and foresight. Determined to help his subjects, he sends his brother-in-law Creon to consult the oracle at Delphi. Upon his return, Creon tells Oedipus that the oracle declared the miasma would be lifted only when the murderer of the previous king, Laius, is found and punished. Oedipus then vows to make "dark things clear" and avenge the wrong that was committed.

As many students who have sat through high school AP English classes know, the dark things only get darker. The wrongdoer, he learns, turns out to have been him: years earlier, Oedipus had killed Laius on a mountain pass, knowing neither his name nor that he was the king of Thebes. Of course, he is also in the dark about his own lineage: not only is Laius his father, but his widow, Jocasta, is his mother. He subsequently becomes ruler of Thebes by wedding his mother—an insight that leads him to gouge out his eyes. As the exiled and blind Oedipus gropes his way from Thebes, Creon reminds him to "crave not mastery in all / For the mastery that raised thee was thy bane and wrought your fall."

In the end, what we find in Sophocles's play is what we find in Thucydides's history. The course of historical events is always in flux; the character of human beings is always fixed. Power blinds us; hubris breaks us; fortune smiles on us, but always with irony. As both writers observe, anger moves people more powerfully than hope, and always in the wrong direction. As the war and pestilence worsen, the Athenians blame Pericles, punishing him for the decisions they had previously praised. Soon after his death, Pericles's place is taken by Alcibiades, who is equally brilliant but utterly self-serving, his greed and arrogance spelling the end of his city. Yet that too—the rise and fall of civilizations—is in the order of things.

But we also find something in Sophocles that we do not find in his contemporary Thucydides: the gods and goddesses. They are utterly absent for the historian, but distantly, direly present for Sophocles. But does this make for a theological distinction without an ethical difference? In the Sophoclean scheme of things, the presence of the gods is hardly more comforting than their absence in the Thucydidean scheme of things. They are not gods who take an interest in humanity, much less an interest in what humanity believes is just and right. They are, instead, gods as the pre-Socratic Heraclitus believed them to be: "Men find some things unjust, other things just; but in the eyes of God all things are beautiful and just and good." This idea of god in fact resembles the one portrayed by another contemporary of Thucydides, but one who, ever so improbably, was sneaked into the Judeo-Christian tradition: the voice from the whirlwind that thunders at Job, "Where were you when I founded Earth?"[10] Remove the voice, keep the whirlwind, and we find ourselves again in the company of Pericles and the plague.

...

On April 13, I was standing at Mrs. M's bedside, trying to land small spoonsful of puréed vegetables into her mouth. Today, as every day, it was touch and go. I had to divine when she was interested or uninterested in eating. Unable to talk, barely able to gesture, her blue eyes—all the more striking against her pale and deeply veined face—were her great means of communication. Or, at least, this is what I told myself. I never really knew if we were on the same page, the same purée, the same planet.

That day, Mrs. M's eyes were fixed on the flat screen, tuned into the daily White House press briefing. Wearing a bright pink, blue, and white scarf tied at her neck, Deborah Birx, the administration's senior health official, was standing in front of a graph. Against a dark blue background were listed the names of countries hardest hit by COVID-19 deaths. Next to each country, placed in descending order of reported deaths per one million, ran a thick white line whose length reflected its comparative mortality rate. Birx pointed to the United States, hovering near the bottom with 11.24 deaths, and remarked: "You can see our case fatality rate is about half to a third of many other countries."

At that point, the president stepped in. In his opening remarks, he had declared that our country had better numbers than any other country, with the possible exception of Germany—"and I think we're as good or better." (The graph numbers behind him, however, showed twice as many Americans dying from COVID-19 as Germans.) Trump now pointed toward the bottom line, occupied by China with just 0.33 reported fatalities. Stretching out his arms, he asked: "And excuse me, but does anybody really believe this number?" To underscore his incredulity, he then repeated his question. Without losing a beat, Birx echoed, in less aggressive language, Trump's skepticism: "I wanted to put China on there so you can see how basically unrealistic this can be."[11]

Looking from the screen to the spoon, I listened to the briefing and watched Mrs. M. I was again trying to read her eyes. Was she listening? If so, what was she thinking? Her eyes grew larger when Trump made his claim about Germany and us; they remained steady during his exchange with Birx. But more than this possible reaction of surprise or skepticism, support or sneers on her part, I cannot report with any confidence. Picking up a kid's carton of strawberry-flavored milk, I wedged open the spout and placed the tip on Mrs. M's lips. Turning her arctic-blue eyes on me, she stared intently as I tipped a few drops into her mouth. Her lips turned upward and formed a faint smile.

Perhaps she was reading my eyes. I was already more than a bit dazed by the cascade of numbers and statistics rumbling off the residence's screens that were more confusing than clarifying. The projections of the various models rarely agreed on how many more confirmed cases and deaths there would be in a week or a month, ranging from the utterly apocalyptic to the merely dire. I kept reminding myself that all models are based as much on assumptions as facts. Take the graph used in that day's briefing. Though I cannot balance a grade book, even I could see that the stats had been stacked. Why were only a handful of European countries, plus China and Iran, on the graph? On a per capita basis, of course, we were doing better than Italy or France. But where were all the other countries? (On that day, it turns out, more than a hundred countries, from Austria to

Singapore, were outperforming the ten countries on the graph.) Moreover, neither Birx nor Trump noted the dramatic disparity in population density—a key element to viral transmission—between those European nations and our own.

By then, I had been with Mrs. M for nearly half an hour. She is both the slowest and the best of eaters, consuming her meals with the relentlessness of a sea turtle lurching from the sea to the beach to lay her eggs. The carton was empty and the purée bowls mostly bare. Putting down the spoon, I dabbed at her mouth with a napkin, picked up her tray, and wished her good night. She was still smiling as I left her room.

…

As with epidemiological models, so too with ancient oracles: you get what you ask for. Just ask Thucydides. He explains that the Athenians, trying to make sense of the plague, rummaged desperately through past events to find missed or misunderstood portents of what was to befall them. They debated, in particular, an ancient prophecy—"A Dorian war shall come and with it pestilence"—that might have anticipated the plague (2.54.3). Was it possible, they wondered, that they had gotten the word "pestilence" wrong? Rather than *limos*, or famine—which is what was originally understood—the oracle in fact said *loimos*, or plague? Could a missing letter have led them, blindly unaware, to this singular event?

Ever the tragedian who wishes to appear neutral, Thucydides does not take sides in the debate. But he cannot help but cite it as an instance of confirmation bias: "The people made their recollection fit in with their sufferings." Ever the historian who knows his fellow Athenians all too well, Thucydides doubts their capacity to measure objectively past or present events: "I suppose, however, that if another Dorian war should ever afterwards come upon us, and a famine should happen to accompany it, the verse will probably be read accordingly" (2.54.3). A very Thucydidean move: a sharp poke done with a poker face.

On occasion, his great predecessor, Herodotus of Halicarnassus, also expressed annoyance with the gullibility of the Athenians. In his *History of the Persian Wars*, he recounts how the sixth century BCE tyrant Pisistratus, banished from Athens, gulled the Athenians into taking him back as ruler. Garbing a statuesque woman in flowing white robes, Pisistratus placed her in a magnificent chariot that was led by heralds announcing that Athena herself was leading the way for the exiled ruler to reassume his position. When the awed Athenians turn their city back over to Pisistratus, Herodotus cannot stop rubbing his eyes. How extraordinary, he exclaims, that a people whose "great cleverness distinguished them from the barbarians" and were "reputed to be the very first in intelligence" could fall for such a "simple-minded ruse."[12]

Yet when it comes to oracles, Herodotus seems—at least to Thucydides—no less gullible. He not only accepts that they have authentic powers of divination, but he also shows proper deference to them. He takes many occasions to remind his listeners, whether human or divine, of his piety. After recounting the questions raised by a particular prophecy, Herodotus makes much ado to disassociate himself from the doubters: "I do not dare myself to speak in denial of oracles, nor will I take that argument from another" (584).

At the same time, he emphasizes that oracular announcements, precisely because they *are* oracular, require a particular kind of intelligence to decrypt. The intelligence, say, of Themistocles, the Athenian leader who was as brilliant as he was bothersome. As the immense Persian army bore down on Athens, Themistocles pushed an interpretation of a Delphic prophecy that seemed outrageous. The oracle's declaration that Athens would be protected by a "wooden wall" was understood by most Athenians as, well, a wooden wall. In haste, they thus began to erect such a wall around the Acropolis (7.143). Yet Themistocles insists they have gotten it wrong. By "wooden wall," the oracle meant the city's triremes: Athens's salvation would be found not on land, but instead on sea. It turned out Themistocles was right: the Persians destroyed the wall on the Acropolis, but the Athenians escaped on their ships and subsequently repelled the invasion.

Herodotus was not alone among his contemporaries in his acceptance of oracles. Belief in the oracles was as widespread as the oracles themselves. Antiquity's equivalent to postmodernity's screen, oracles were everywhere and just about any event, from the marvelous to the mundane, was ripe for reading. As the classicist Michael Scott writes, "the Greek world was filled with a constant hum of divine communication."[13] What astonishes with Thucydides is his seeming indifference to this omnipresent hum. Not only are the gods absent from his account, but oracles are reduced to walk-on roles. For every three references to oracles and prophecies in Herodotus, there is but one in Thucydides.[14] Moreover, when he does refer to the oracles, it is often to point out how they misled those who consulted them.

But there's something of a rub. Before he became a historian, Thucydides was, like Pericles, a general or *strategos*. As an Athenian strategist in fifth century BCE, he could no more avoid the use of divination than an American strategist in the twenty-first century CE could avoid the use of game theory. Every time Thucydides led an attack, Hugh Bowden argues, he must have overseen sacrifices where the animal's entrails would be studied, perhaps by himself, before deciding on a course of action.[15] Is it possible that Thucydides does not dismiss the power of oracles, but instead dismisses the power of human beings to rightly read them? Or, instead, that just as there are no atheists in foxholes, there are no atheists on triremes?

...

Thucydides concludes his account of the plague with a lapidary phrase: "Such was the nature of the calamity, and heavily did it weigh on the Athenians; death raging within the city and devastation without" (2.54). Calamity indeed. The first wave of the plague was followed by others that swept through Athens until 426 BCE. Though the estimates vary, as many as 100,000 men, women, and children—approximately one-third of the city's population of 300,000, including metics, or foreign residents, and slaves—may have died from the disease. It is possible to calculate the military costs. Thucydides states that the lives of 4,000 hoplites, or foot soldiers, as well as 300 cavalrymen were taken by the plague (3.87). In relative terms, according to the military historian Victor Davis Hanson, these losses equal those at the battles of the Somme or Stalingrad. Hanson also observes that Athens never again fielded the same number of soldiers that it had at the war's beginning, a fatal factor in closely fought and lost battles at Delium and Mantinea.[16] The loss of workers, which hobbled the city's economy, and the loss of men and women of childbearing age, which staggered its demography, undoubtedly contributed to Athens's final defeat in 404 BCE.

It is impossible, however, to calculate or comprehend the psychological costs wrought by the plague. Eerily, the generation of Athenians that comes of age between the start and end of the Peloponnesian War resembles the generation of French that spans *les années creuses*, or the "hollow years" between the First and Second World Wars. As with the young French, who were reminded of the first war's cost by the sight of the *gueules cassées*, or "broken faces" of wounded veterans, young Athenians must have been familiar with plague survivors who had been disfigured or crippled. These kinds of wounds—arousing apprehension, not veneration—did not inspire well-spoken orations, but instead unspoken dread. Not only did the unanticipated appearance of the plague take Pericles's life, but it also took away the city's confidence in the rational leadership he embodied. Those who subsequently rose to power were either violent mediocrities like Cleon who played on fear or self-serving demagogues like Alcibiades who exploited greed. What had been the best of times, engraved in Pericles's funeral oration, had become the worst of times, expressed by the words of the Athenian commander in the Melian Dialogue: "The strong do what they can, the weak suffer what they must" (5.89).

Whoever that unnamed commander was, he did not speak those words. They are, instead, the words of a different commander—Thucydides. Among the few things we know about Thucydides is that he served, like Pericles, as a *strategos*. In Book 4, we learn he led a naval expedition to parry the Spartan advance on Amphipolis, an Athenian ally, in 424 BCE. In a few terse lines, Thucydides recounts that Amphipolis fell before the fleet of seven triremes could arrive; he then returns to his narrative. What we do not learn until Book 5 is that the Athenian assembly, alarmed by Amphipolis's fall, placed the blame with Thucydides and not the winds. They exiled him from Athens—an exile, he laconically notes, that gave him the sudden leisure and perspective to write his history.

It also gave the twentieth-century Polish poet Zbigniew Herbert a subject for his poem "Why the Classics." This episode, Herbert writes, is dropped "like a pin in a forest," buried in the midst of "long speeches of chiefs / battles sieges plague / dense net of intrigues of diplomatic endeavors." How sharp a contrast, he continues, with his own age and leaders. "Generals of the most recent wars / if a similar affair happens to them / whine on their knees before posterity / praise their heroism and innocence." The bleakness that imbues the poem, first published in English in 1968, reflects our time as much as his. But while Thucydides does not leave much room for hope, he leaves even less room for despair. The city of Athens fell, but its virtues of intelligence and integrity, civic-mindedness and open-mindedness abide. These are virtues that will be repeatedly eclipsed over time and place, but never extinguished. Perhaps this is why the classics and why this classic is a possession for all time.

2

MARCUS AURELIUS AND THE ANTONINE PLAGUE

> In the beginning of this great plague—if only it would end!—a certain youth, who had been ill for nine days, suffered from ulcers erupting on his whole body, just like almost everyone else who survived.
> GALEN

> Soon you will have forgotten all things: soon all things will have forgotten you.
> MARCUS AURELIUS

In 162 CE, an ambitious physician, Aelius Galenus, settled in Rome. Better known to posterity by his Anglicized name Galen, his choice of professions reflected his place of birth, the city of Pergamum. This thriving cultural and commercial hub in western Asia Minor was famed for its great altar to Zeus, with its frieze of the battle between the gods and giants stretching a hundred feet, and its library, filled with 200,000 scrolls and second only to the library of Alexandria. Yet it was perhaps most renowned for its temple to Asclepius, the Roman god of healing. Just six years before Galen's birth in 129 CE, the emperor Hadrian's visit to the temple inspired a great refurbishing of the sacred grounds. It resulted in an elegant complex of buildings that included a theater, a library, and a grand hall for the thousands of pilgrims who came to supplicate the god. And, of course, there were state-of-the-art latrines.[1]

For Galen, sacred supplication was well and good, but no substitute for scientific investigation. By the time he arrived in Rome, Galen had been preceded by the reputation as someone who dissected his opponents' claims with the same formidable skill that he dissected dead and living animals. Widely traveled and widely read, Galen had already, by the time he reached Rome, authored dozens of the towering pile of medical and scientific works he would eventually leave behind him. The works abound with keen observations of not just the patients he had treated and works he had read, but also the places he had visited. Despite the many marvels he had seen, none could have been more marvelous or monstrous than Rome. It was, he wrote, "a city with such a throng of people, that the rhetor Polemo praised it as the epitome of the world."[2]

When it comes to determining the size of ancient Rome's population, historians are mostly left tossing darts at numbers. But even if the default estimate of one million inhabitants errs by a hundred thousand or so, Rome's population size was as unprecedented as were the public health concerns it presented. Few homes were connected to sewers, while the sewers themselves were overwhelmed by the amount of waste they received. The repeated injunctions against littering thoroughfares with human excrement—or, for that matter, animal and human corpses—suggests that, in effect, the city's streets *were* the city's sewers. Even Rome's vaunted public baths, supplied by the intricate system of aqueducts, shunted dirty water into the streets. Like the rest of the city's repellent sludge, this heated and dirtied drain-off emptied into the Tiber River.

Add to this the density of living quarters—most Romans lived in multistory dwellings called *insulae*—and the material precarity of their lives: Rome was what the historian Kyle Harper describes as a "pathogen bomb."[3] The patients seen by Galen were afflicted by the dizzying array of diseases cultivated in the city's foul streets and buildings. Malaria ravaged the city, as did typhoid and hepatitis, tuberculosis and leprosy, and sundry diarrheal diseases. Yet this great array of maladies, while chronic, were not cataclysmic. Their presence was constant, but they never threatened to overwhelm the city. Like highway fatalities in modern cities, bacteriological fatalities in ancient cities were an unfortunate, but not unsurprising part of life—until, that is, 166 CE.

...

The year before Galen moved to Rome, a new emperor had moved into the imperial palace. With the death of his adoptive father Antoninus Pius in 161 CE, Marcus Aurelius became the empire's ruler. Though long groomed for the position, the forty-year-old prince was loath to accept the position, overcome by a sincere and deep *horror imperii.*[4] For this reason, in part, Marcus insisted upon sharing rule with his adoptive brother Lucius Verus. By both accepting and dividing the role of emperor, the forty-year-old Marcus fulfilled the wishes of Hadrian, the same emperor who visited Pergamum. During the last years of his reign, the sickly Hadrian had created a daring scheme of succession, choosing the aptly named Pius as his successor, but also insisting that Pius name Marcus and Lucius as *his* successors. Despite its Rube Goldbergian nature, the plan worked so well that Marcus's name, not Hadrian's, has won the most renown.

In her stunning work of contemporary fiction based on historical facts, *Memoirs of Hadrian*, the French novelist Marguerite Yourcenar reimagines the dying Roman emperor reflecting on his life. Relating these reflections in a (very) long letter to Marcus Aurelius, Yourcenar's Hadrian explains to his eventual successor why he had chosen him. He had, he writes, "concerned myself with the education of this almost too sober little boy, helping your father to choose the best masters for you. Verus, the Most Veracious: I used to play on your name; you are perhaps the only being who has never lied to me. I have seen you read with passion the writings of the philosophers, and clothe yourself in harsh wool, sleeping on the bare floor and forcing your somewhat frail body to all the mortifications of the Stoics . . . I divine in you the presence of a genius which is not necessarily that of a statesman; the world will doubtless be forever the better off, however, for having once seen such qualities operating in conjunction with supreme authority . . . I believe that I may be giving mankind the only chance it will ever have to realize Plato's dream, to see a philosopher pure of heart ruling over his fellow men."[5]

Yourcenar's depiction of the young Marcus Aurelius is mostly true to what ancient and modern historians have written. Even when she errs—for example, while Marcus did try at the age of twelve to sleep on the bare floor, his mother forced him to instead sleep on a simple bed covered with animal skins—Yourcenar does so on behalf of a deeper truth. Already as a boy, Marcus gravitated to philosophy, evincing an air of gravitas. Once placed in the imperial line, Marcus avidly pursued these interests. Among his tutors was Apollonius of Chalcedon, a well-known Stoic philosopher. By way of asserting his credentials, when Antoninus Pius ordered him to come to the imperial palace to teach the young Marcus, Apollonius replied: "The master should not come to the pupil, but the pupil to the master." Though Antoninus laughed over the exchange—"It was easier for Apollonius to come from Chalcedon to Rome," he joked, "than from his house in Rome to mine"—the grave and young Marcus nevertheless went to his teacher. Much later, he recalled that among the lessons he learned from Apollonius was "moral freedom, the certainty to ignore the dice of fortune, and have no other perspective, even for a moment, than that of reason alone; to be always the same man, unchanged in sudden pain, in the loss of a child, in lingering sickness"[6] (Book 1, 8).

Yet the mentor who left the deepest impression on Marcus was not Apollonius, but instead his mentor Quintus Junius Rusticus. A man of state, Rusticus was the grandson of Arulenus Rusticus, a senator who, having denounced the excesses of the emperor Domitian, was assassinated for his pains. Rusticus embodied the philosophical principles taught by Apollonius. It was Rusticus's bearing—his very being—that daily reminded Marcus, as he himself observed, that he "wanted correction and treatment for my character." By the simplicity of his mentor's way of speaking and writing, Marcus learned "not to be diverted into a taste for rhetoric" and to avoid "delivering my own little moral sermons or presenting a glorified picture of the ascetic" (Book 1, 7).

But this was not all Marcus received from Rusticus. In the *Meditations*, he ends his encomium on a telling note. Thanks to Rusticus, Marcus writes, he "encountered the *Discourses* of Epictetus, to which he introduced me with his own copy." Rusticus was indeed a man of state, but one guided by the same philosophy that spurred his grandfather's opposition to Domitian. Not only was Epictetus also feared by Domitian—who exiled him to the Greek city of Nicopolis—but more than any other thinker, he also shaped Marcus's understanding of Stoicism. That one was a freed slave and the other a Roman emperor was, quite literally, a matter of indifference to both men. Was not the core principle of this philosophy, after all, the belief in the dignity of reason in all human beings?

...

In 166 CE, just four years after moving to Rome, Galen tried to slip out of the city as quietly and quickly as possible. Why on earth would he abandon so promising a career choice? In his autobiographical text *On Prognosis*, he gives two reasons for stealing away "like a runaway slave": the resentment his successes had ignited among his peers and the rumors that the emperor would command his presence.[7] Making one's way as a physician in ancient Rome was a cutthroat business, a contest that Galen—who, after all, was a virtuoso at vivisection—had proven especially skilled. By 166, he had dazzled the Roman elites by a string of medical coups, most recently curing the pelvic abscess of the wife of the Roman senator and ex-consul Titus Flavius Boethus.

It was not surprising that news of Galen's achievements reached the imperial palace. What is surprising, though, is that he did not welcome the rumors with open arms. For Galen, there could have been no greater honor than to be named "physician to the emperor," especially when the emperor was Marcus Aurelius. Just as Galen thought of himself as a physician who was also a philosopher, he knew that Marcus thought of himself as a philosopher who was also an emperor. Given these attractions, Galen might have done what any socially adept Roman would do: step back from a proffered honor in order to better pounce upon it.

Yet there is a third possibility for fleeing Rome, one offered by Galen himself. In another treatise—titled, aptly enough, *On My Own Books*—he declares that "the plague" drove him from the imperial capital. Yet, as the historian Susan Mattern notes, there is something odd about Galen's claim. If plague was the reason he was flying from Rome, then his ultimate destination, Pergamum, led him straight to, and not away from, the pestilence. This mass mortality event was approaching the largely unwitting Rome from the east, a path that went through Pergamum. As Galen well knew, the plague had just struck Smyrna, now known as Izmir and located in western Turkey. As Mattern suggests, Galen's departure may well have been a frantic attempt to help family and friends in Pergamum, which was a mere sixty miles from Smyrna.

Succeeding in leaving Rome without arousing attention, Galen reached Pergamum and discovered that his help was not needed: the city had, for the moment, dodged the disease. In no hurry to return to Rome, Galen decided to remain there, peacefully spending the next two years in his native city. His peace was shattered in 168 CE, however, with the arrival of the dreaded missive carrying the news that Marcus Aurelius commanded his presence. By then, however, Marcus was no longer present in Rome. Instead, he and Lucius were returning to the city from the wars they had led against the Sarmatians to the east and the Marcomanni, a Germanic tribe, to the north. Despite his many experiences as a traveler, Galen could not have welcomed the prospect of leaving his home and joining the emperor at a military camp. But what could he do? As he wrote laconically, "By necessity, I went to Rome."[8]

Traveling north, he reached the town of Aquileia, situated at the head of the Adriatic Sea. It was there that he may have met both emperors, but most certainly met what he called "the plague." Its onslaught was so intense, Galen writes, "that the emperors immediately fled to Rome with a few soldiers, while most of us struggled for a long time to stay alive, and a great many died—not only because of the plague, but also because these things were happening in the middle of winter." As it turned out, Lucius never reached Rome—the plague took him in transit—while Marcus survived. Alone as emperor, his task was to maintain the empire in the face of the twinned crises of war and plague. If he was to do so, he had to maintain empire over himself. What better way to do so than by writing? It was for this reason that, in the midst of war and plague, Marcus began his *Meditations.*

...

Early in the Hollywood blockbuster *Gladiator*, the movie's hero Maximus—the Roman general played by Russell Crowe—is, like Galen, commanded to appear at the emperor's tent. Upon entering, the battered Maximus, having just defeated an invading Germanic tribe, finds himself alone with the tent's occupant, Marcus Aurelius. Played by Richard Harris, he is bowed over a sheaf of parchment, intently scribbling. Silence ensues. After what seems an eternity, the weary-faced and bleary-eyed emperor looks up, wipes his nose, and asks an uneasy Maximus why they are there. By "they," Marcus means Rome; by "there," he means the dark and mysterious expanse on the empire's northernmost frontier. The answer is obvious, Maximus believes: "For the glory of the Roman Empire." And, no doubt, he thought this is what Marcus was doing at that very moment: maintaining that same empire through the writing of directives. Adjudicating legal cases and assigning imperial titles, commissioning buildings and commanding armies. But could Marcus, at that moment, have been busy maintaining a different kind of empire? He drops a hint when, turning to Maximus, he asks how the world will speak his name, Marcus Aurelius, in years to come. Before the puzzled general can reply, Marcus adds, "As a philosopher?"

The answer, of course, is a thousand times "yes." Despite the Aurelian column—the massive marble monument that towers nearly one hundred feet over tourists in Rome, celebrating Marcus's military victories—and despite the imposing bronze equestrian statue of Marcus, radiating imperial power and confidence now standing in the Capitoline Museum—the world remembers Marcus Aurelius as a philosopher. Yet as a philosopher of a particular sort, one who held empire not just over much of the world, but who also held empire over his inner world—a state of mind that requires a special kind of exercise, one that the late historian of ancient philosophy, Pierre Hadot, has called "spiritual exercises."

Hadot was among the first scholars to suggest that the ancient schools of philosophy were radically different from their modern counterparts. At universities today, students take courses in order to be informed about this or that branch of philosophical inquiry. Whether the field is epistemology or phenomenology, whether the subject is science or syntax, contemporary philosophers teach the finer points in their particular fields. At the end of a class, students leave the room replete with axioms and arguments, while professors return to their offices depleted from having repeated what they have taught many times before. But neither student nor teacher leaves the room lastingly different from the way they were when they entered.

This response to philosophy, Hadot believed, would have surprised a student of philosophy two millennia ago. Whether the school was Aristotelian or Epicurean, Stoic or Cynic, a student did not seek to be informed, but instead to be formed; not to train for a livelihood, but to change his—or, indeed, her—life. Even in our therapeutic age, where self-help sections at bookstores are often the fullest and most frequented, this claim can still jolt. By institutional inertia or individual habit, we still cling to the modern connotation of philosophy—namely, various fields of arcane knowledge often written in obscure language on matters that have no obvious implications for our everyday lives.

Yet, this was not at all the case with ancient schools of philosophy. As Hadot argues, students during the Hellenistic era attended a particular school "because of the kind of life that its philosophy offered."[9] Each school offered a *technê*, or art, with which the students could shape themselves. The claim made by Epictetus applied to all the schools of philosophy: "Just as wood is the material of the carpenter, bronze that of the statue maker, so each individual's life is the subject matter of the art of living."[10] As a result, Epictetus encouraged his students "to have a pen always in hand in order to write down the principles of Stoicism."[11]

When Maximus steps into Marcus's tent, the emperor may have been in the midst of sculpting a self—a never-ending task that requires constant attention. In this instance, though, his tool was not clay or knife, but instead parchment and pen. With these tools, the philosopher engaged in what the Greeks called *askêsis*, or exercise—more particularly, a form of ethical exercise. Crucially, Epictetus did not mean students should spend their time reading the writings of Stoic sages. To the contrary, he found this activity a waste of time and effort. Such an activity is no more a true exercise than, say, watching a tennis match rather than playing a match of tennis. Reading a philosophical text might fill our minds, but it will not change our lives. Such works are mostly designed to memorize, not interiorize; they might inform us, but they rarely if ever *form* us.

Upon Antoninus Pius's death, Marcus had become Imperator Caesar Marcus Aurelius Antoninus Augustus—a title that endowed him with not just awesome earthly powers but also divine status. Given this transformation, as well as the strict protocols of the court, Marcus could not expect to have a candid conversation with anyone other than himself. But he never lost sight of Epictetus's urgent exhortations. They gave him a salutary shake when he needed it. This helps explain the nature of his book, the *Meditations*. It was meant for his eyes alone—hence the title on the Greek manuscript, since lost, used for the first printed edition: *Ta eis heauton*, or *Addresses to Himself*. Think of it as a series of memos whose language always changes, but whose truths are few and never changing.

...

In his sweeping account of the impact of climate and disease on the Roman Empire, Kyle Harper asserts that what came to be called the Antonine Plague was "unlike anything anyone had ever witnessed . . . its arrival marked the beginning of a new age."[12] This new disease, transmitted directly between humans, was qualitatively different from those maladies, like malaria and typhus, that had taken up residency in Rome and its empire. Though Galen variously calls the disease the "plague," "great plague," and "long plague," he never gives it a more specific name. As was the case with Thucydides half a millennium earlier, "plague" remained a one-size-fits-all term used in ancient Rome for mass mortality events. As for its cause, while the number of candidates is dizzying, ranging from typhus and cholera to malaria and the bubonic plague, the historical consensus has settled on smallpox. This largely conforms to Galen's description of the disease, in particular the appearance of dark red rashes that would ulcerate much of the body. At the same time, nowhere does Galen mention facial scarring, the most dreaded symptom of smallpox in later times, or raging fever. Most telling, though, is the phrase that does appear from time to time in his otherwise cool and objective descriptions of the disease: "If only it would end!"[13]

Galen was not alone to explode in despair: archaeologists have discovered evidence of appeals and supplications made to Apollo, the god of pestilence, from all corners of the empire for an end to the plague. Emissaries from towns and cities traveled to various shrines of Apollo, where they were told by the oracles that they were "not alone in being injured by the destructive miseries of a deadly plague." While little solace was offered in such pronouncements, the oracles also suggested a few prescriptions. Along with the usual fumigation and ritual lustration, a common oracular suggestion was to erect a statue of Apollo—portrayed with his bow drawn, aiming "his arrows from afar at the unfertile plague"—outside the city walls.[14]

In Rome, spiraling mortality rates sparked chaos at cemeteries, with the hijacking of sepulchers and beggaring of poor Romans who could not afford proper burials for family members. In response, Marcus issued an edict that forbade the commandeering of burial sites and provided state aid to pay funeral expenses for the poor.[15] More worrisome was the pandemic's scythe-like decimation of the Roman legions, leading Marcus to replenish the ranks by enlisting gladiators and slaves who were promised manumission in return for their service. Moreover, the work at imperial silver mines seems to have ground to a halt, convulsing Rome's fiscal system. With the plague smothering commercial activity, tax revenue suffered so greatly that, in 169 CE, Marcus auctioned off possessions from the imperial palace to make up for the deficit.[16]

Unfortunately, this handful of documented events are like messages in bottles floating atop a sea we cannot plumb. It may well be, some Roman historians argue, that the very absence of documents and inscriptions from this period reveals the shattering impact of the pandemic. Whether their case is conclusive may never be known, but what can be said with certainty is that the paucity of written and archaeological evidence has long divided historians over the true extent of the economic and social consequences of the Antonine Plague.[17] The middle ground claimed by the demographer Bruce Frier—the plague "ushered in, or immensely complicated, a host of social and economic problems"—nevertheless reflects the event's potentially seismic impact, one with vast consequences for most every aspect of life during Marcus's reign.[18] While historians will never know the exact number of deaths across the empire caused by the pandemic—the estimates range from 2 percent (1.5 million) to 30 percent (25 million)—few would argue with Harper's conclusion that it was "in absolute terms, the worst disease event in human history up to that time."[19]

...

I spent the first Saturday of April at the residence dressed as the Easter Bunny. What choice did I have? It was a week before Easter and the director, a stately and slim woman in her sixties, impressed upon me that the sight of a six-foot-two pink rabbit would bring joy to the residents. I nearly replied, "But I'm Jewish," but instead said I'd be glad to hop the hallways.

It turns out that hopping while your body is wrapped in a thick polyester rug is not all that easy. It is even less so when your head is encased in a heavy plastic globe with two holes to see through. Besides, as the globe swiveled and jiggled with each hop, what I really needed was a radar dish instead of eyeholes. But hop I did: into carts and walls, but fortunately not into wheelchairs or nurses. The more I hopped, the more my shirt and slacks under the costume grew damp, the more my vision blurred with a curtain of sweat lowering over my eyes. But the more I hopped, the more staff asked to take selfies with me, the more I heard laughs and chatter, the more I believed I was being useful.

When I hopped into Room 232, I tried to fix my eyes on its resident, Mrs. M, a tiny and thin, clear-minded and clipped-tongue octogenarian who, though listed as a hospice resident, was always seated bolt-upright in her chair. When I finally aligned my eyes with the holes, I saw a frail and frightened woman wrapped in a brown shawl and staring slightly above my right shoulder. How could I have forgotten that Mrs. M is also blind? I quickly pulled off my bunny head and explained why I had made such a ruckus. She relaxed when she heard my voice and, her eyes fixed at a place not quite where I was standing, assured me that I must be a sight. You've no idea what a sight, I answered, sponging off my face with a bunny arm. Seeing the half-eaten lunch tray on her table, I asked if she was still hungry. No, she replied. Could I then take her tray, I wondered? In response, I got a polite "No. I might be hungry again in a bit." With a sharp smile, she added: "Now you need to hop to the next room."

And so, I continued to hop, next stopping at the room of Mr. Mc, who had worked as a researcher and, as he told me several times, had a PhD in chemistry. When a fellow staff person told him that I taught at the university, Mr. Mc embraced me as a fellow academic, sharing gossip from his long-gone days as a doctoral student. When I removed my bunny head, he smiled and waved me closer. Staring hard at me through his steel-rimmed glasses, he asked conspiratorially, "Have you read the article on turpentine?" Puzzled, I replied, "Turpentine?" He nodded his head: "You need to make the time." Assuring him I would, I glanced at the flat screen on the wall by his bed: the daily White House press conference was about to start. I wiped my brow, put my head back on, and continued on my Easter rounds.

As I hopped toward the nurses' station—an oblong rampart resembling the cockpit of the *Starship Enterprise* behind which nurses swiveled in chairs, staring at screens and murmuring into phones—President Trump's thick voice had already begun to spill into the hallway from the rooms. I turned into Mrs. W's room, hoping to escape the voice. A thin woman with a narrow face, livid complexion, and wild mop of gray hair, Mrs. W was one of my favorite residents. Dementia had established a beachhead in her brain, but she struggled mightily to keep it from moving any further. Every day she greeted me with a loud "Okey-dokey"—a sign that she still recognized me, a sign she still recognized herself.

Reclining in her bed at the far side of the room, bathed in the light slanting through the window, she clapped when she saw me. "Marvelous," she cried. "But is it okey-dokey?" I asked. "Very okey-dokey," Mrs. W blurted. I asked about her three grown sons, including Stuart the doctor, whom she spoke about most often. They were all fine, I learned. "Why, I just spoke to Stuart the other day," she added. How nice, I replied, passing over the fact that she told me every day that she spoke to Stuart just the other day. My attention was drawn to the screen as President Trump, who had recently, but fleetingly, it soon turned out, acknowledged the grim forecasts of his coronavirus task force. "There will be a lot of death," he intoned from behind his lectern in the Rose Garden. Yet, he also held out hope that come Easter Sunday, just one week away, churches could open as long as they practiced "great separation."

While Trump talked, I glanced at the dashboard on the bottom of the screen. This is the name given to the row of numbers that measure how quickly we are approaching the epidemiological cliff edge. As of today, Texas had registered 6,100 cases of COVID-19. It doesn't seem like much in a state that prides itself on being the biggest in most every way. The number of positive cases, were they housed there, would be dwarfed inside our famous megachurch, Lakewood Church, the former home to the Houston Rockets that seats more than 16,000 congregants. As for the number of deaths, 105, they could probably fit comfortably in what was once the locker rooms. What the dashboard did not list, though, was the latest projection by the Institute for Health Metrics and Evaluation, which forecast that by early 2021, Texas would tally 32,000 cases of COVID-related deaths. A lot of death—more than enough to fill two morning services at Lakewood.

Mrs. W was staring at the screen too. With the bunny head in one hand, I waved one of the floppy ears at her with the other hand. She clapped her hands, laughed, and held up a letter sitting on her table. "I got a letter today." "Wow!" I replied. "Letters are so rare nowadays." She nodded her head, adding, "It's from a funeral home." After an awkward pause, we looked at one another and smiled. Okey-dokey, indeed.

...

For a man who, as a boy, chose to sleep on the floor rather than a bed, holding a garage sale of palatial furniture and decor to citizens could not have cost Marcus much sleep. After all, he told himself that it was possible to "live in a palace without feeling the need for bodyguards or fancy uniforms, candelabra, statues, or the other trappings of suchlike pomp" (Book 1, 17). At the same time, though, the reason for the auction weighed on him whether at the palace in Rome or, as Marcus writes in Book 2, "among the Quadi on the River Gran." How could the plague not have worried him? It was not only whipsawing through the ranks of his legions, but had also carried off his adoptive brother and co-emperor, Lucius Verus—he "whose character could spur me to care for myself" (Book 1, 17)—leaving that particular self alone to direct the empire.

Yet, without his brother and in the midst of these extraordinary responsibilities, Marcus nevertheless strove to care for that self, one that was vulnerable to plagues of a different order. More dangerous than the arrows dispatched by Apollo, he insisted, were the falsehoods and deceptions displayed by men. "Has your experience not yet persuaded you to shun this plague? Because the corruption of the mind is much more a plague than any such contaminating change in the surrounding air we breathe. The latter infects animate creatures in their animate nature: the former infects human beings in their humanity" (Book 9, 2).

Without a brother to remind him or a teacher to instruct him, Marcus became his own reminder and instructor. As Epictetus urged his students, "Become, yourself, both your own pupil and your own teacher."[20] In effect, Marcus *qua* teacher assigns homework to Marcus *qua* student: the task of writing to himself. Late in his own life, the philosopher Michel Foucault made the same discovery in regard to the impact of writing on the self. In his essay "Self-Writing," he observes that as an ethical exercise, writing to and for oneself "works not just on actions, but more precisely, on thought: the constraint that the presence of others exerts in the domain of conduct, writing will exert in the domain of the inner impulses."[21]

For Foucault, the reason to practice such writing is to care for one's self. But this is not at all the case with the Stoics, who believed the reason for such exercises was reason itself. Rather than the care for oneself, the *technê* of writing to oneself is, first and foremost, to care for others by aligning one's actions with *logos*. This Greek word, which has bled in countless ways into English, means many things, ranging from "word" through "speech" to "reason." All of these variations are at play when Marcus uses the word, but they all derive their purpose from the most important meaning of *logos*: the rational or divine principle that oversees the cosmic scheme of things. It is our capacity both to reason and to express the results of our reasoning that makes us *logos*'s witting collaborators.

This collaboration is crucial, in part, because it allows us to distinguish between those things which, depending upon us, we can control and those things which, depending on external causes, are beyond our control. The Stoic assigns the latter to the realm of things indifferent—namely, events that unfold according to what we might call logical design. As for the former—which we can call the empire of reason—it is the means to make this distinction. As the *logos*, so the world goes—as well as you, me, and everyone else. We can do so either willingly or unwillingly, wisely or unwisely, but at the behest of *logos* we must go all the same. It is through the use of our individual reason that we grasp the principle of reason at work in the world and ourselves.

For Marcus, this is cause for celebration, not agitation. "If mind is common to us all, then we have reason also in common—that which makes us rational beings. If so, then common too is the reason which dictates what we should or should not do. If so, then law is common to us all" (Book 4, 4). Through the application of her reason, the Stoic can freely choose to articulate her actions in accordance with the will of Reason. That this decision can be freely willed is crucial. "Consider who you are," Epictetus reminded his students. "First of all, you are a human being, that is, one who has nothing more ruling than choice, and all else subordinate to that, but that itself without slavery or subjection."[22] And so, paradoxically, it is by choosing voluntary servitude to what Marcus calls "the directing Mind" that the Stoic most fully realizes his freedom.

Think of our situation as akin to that of a dog tied to a cart—a favorite image of the founder of Stoicism, Zeno of Citium. The leash allows the dog a limited degree of movement; ultimately, however, the dog must go where the cart goes. Inevitably, some dogs nevertheless try to go in the opposite direction; flailing and failing, they are, no less inevitably, forced to follow the cart. The wise dog, Zeno declares, is the one who "makes its spontaneous action coincide with necessity" and trots by the cart's side. By the same token, the wise human being is not one who rages against and resists the direction taken by logos, but instead one who adjusts her actions accordingly. In effect, the Stoic sage teaches us to trot alongside the world—a choice that will not just spare us useless exertion but also spur us to exert ourselves usefully for one another.

This is not an easy task. Time and again, Marcus exhorts himself to do better when he deals with, as he writes, those madmen who expect figs in winter (Book 11, 33). Upon waking every day, he reminds himself that he will "meet people who are meddling, ungrateful, aggressive, treacherous, malicious, unsocial" (Book 2, 1). This entry, the first in Book 2, was written, as Marcus notes, "among the Quadi on the River Gran." While he might have had barbarians in mind, he knew that such qualities were, unhappily, as universal as reason. In another entry, in which the identity of the individual Marcus unloads on is unknown, he reveals just how difficult a task exercising reason can be when confronted by those who refuse to reason: "A black character, an effeminate, unbending character, the character of a brute or dumb animal: infantile, stupid, fraudulent, coarse, mercenary, despotic" (Book 4, 28). In the great unfolding of *logos*, the unreasonable as well as the reasonable are picked up and carried off. The unreasonable do not understand what is happening, of course. But when their paths collide with those who do understand—emperors included—the latter's challenge, even if bruised or berated, is "to teach him kindly and show him what he has failed to see. If you can't do that, blame yourself—or perhaps not even yourself" (Book 10, 4). Is it possible, though, that kindness has its limits, especially when strangers depend upon it?

...

Nearly one hundred feet in height and standing in the middle of Rome's Piazza Colonna, the Aurelian Column was begun toward the end of Marcus's life and completed under the reign of his son, Commodus. A series of friezes spiraling upward from the base of the monument leads the gaze to the very top, where a massive statue of Marcus Aurelius once stood. (In the late sixteenth century, Pope Sixtus V had the likeness of the pagan emperor replaced by a statue of Saint Paul.) The column's twenty-eight marble blocks were stacked upon one another in order to celebrate Marcus's victories over the Sarmatians and Marcomanni—victories that are narrated by the friezes. Nearly half of the 116 scenes depicted on the column deal with either battle- or war-related violence. Blurred and blemished over more than a millennium, these scenes were also restored at the order of Sixtus. With the restoration came the revelation, in details that can freeze the soul, of what happens when a Stoic philosopher makes war.

The message conveyed by the carvings, beginning with the army's crossing of the Danube over pontoon bridges, is of inexorability. Sheer inevitability. Advancing shoulder to shoulder, shield to shield, the marching legionnaires signal overwhelming force—a force as all-encompassing and all-powerful as divine reason itself. The friezes do not show the Romans battling the barbarians as much as simply bulldozing over them. German villages are razed, villagers are killed; German warriors are taken prisoner, the prisoners are beheaded; the faces of the Germans radiate fear, the faces of the Romans radiate fortitude. At times, barbarians are forced to behead one another; at other times, legionnaires do the beheading. In one frieze, an erect Marcus oversees executions; in another frieze, a seated Marcus receives severed heads from his soldiers.

In Book 8, Marcus asks himself if he has "ever seen a severed hand or foot, or a head cut off and lying some way away from the rest of the body." He knows the answer: during the last ten years of his life, most of which Marcus spent in the northern military camps, he had ample opportunity to see limbs and heads shorn from their bodies on the battlefield. War is always a fierce affair, but these northern wars were particularly brutal. Whereas the campaigns of his predecessor Trajan were fueled by conquest, those led by Marcus were fired by revenge and retribution. The Marcomanni tribes north of the Danube, which had long coexisted with Rome, launched these wars by bursting across the imperial frontiers and, to the horror of Rome, pushing into Italy proper. The shock wave that swept over the empire was quickly overtaken by an even greater wave of fury. In a shuffling of the values of the *mos maiorum*, it was *auctoritas*, not *clementia*, that was now embraced. As Germanicus said of an earlier instance of German treachery—Arminius's annihilation of three Roman legions at the Battle of Teutoburg in 9 CE—"There is no use in taking prisoners; only the destruction of the race will end the war."[23] Though his account must be taken with a few grains of salt, the contemporary historian Cassius Dio claims that Marcus's attitude toward the Parthian tribes was as severe as Germanicus's toward the German tribes. "He wished to exterminate them utterly, for they were still strong at this time and had done the Romans great harm."[24]

The soldiers climbing toward the top of the column reflect Rome's need to act with overwhelming *auctoritas* against these rebellious tribes. No doubt Marcus, though he had never before seen battle, understood the necessity to devastate the Marcomanni. No doubt he must also have recalled the warning about "striking down the haughty" given to Aeneas, the mythical founder of Rome, by his father Anchises in Virgil's epic poem *The Aeneid*. As the friezes reveal, this is what Marcus's armies did: they struck down the German invaders haughty enough to have invaded Italy. Yet Marcus had undoubtedly also remembered the rest of Anchises's instruction to his son: "Spare the conquered." Tragically, Aeneas fails to do this at the poem's climax. When his defeated opponent, Turnus, stretches out his hand and begs Aeneas to "lay down [his] hatred," Aeneas at first wavers. But when Aeneas is suddenly reminded that Turnus had killed his friend Pallas, he is consumed by "hideous rage" and thrusts his sword into his suppliant's chest.

We can never know, of course, the accuracy of the anonymous artist's depiction of Marcus. What, though, if he captured not the emperor's actual countenance but what that countenance *should* have been? Gazing at Marcus's face as he receives the decapitated heads—carried by the soldiers like huge beets ripped from the ground—I see furrows and lines, but neither wavering nor wrath. What might he have been thinking at this moment? Surely not what he wrote, either before or after this particular battle, in his *Meditations*: "Kindness is invincible . . . What can the most aggressive man do to you if you continue to be kind to him? If, as opportunity arises, you gently admonish him and take your time to re-educate him at the very moment when he is trying to do you harm?" (Book 11, 18, 9). Perhaps he instead recalled, as he looked at the bodiless heads, what he also wrote, either before or after this moment, in his *Meditations*: "Every hour of the day give vigorous attention, as a Roman and as a man, to the performance of the task at hand . . . with dispassionate justice" (Book 2, 5). I look closer at Marcus's lips; they are not downturned, but instead turned slightly upward in a mild smile. His face suggests a kind of joy—not the sort shared by his soldiers, but instead shared by his fellow Stoics, the kind of joy that, for Seneca, is always "a stern matter."[25] It is the joy of giving close attention to the matter at hand. In this instance, though, the matter at hand is another's head in hand.

…

One striking aspect to the *Meditations* is not what's there, but what *isn't* there. Though written in a time of war and plague, there is scarce mention of either one or the other. As for war, Marcus offers a handful of fleeting references—"life is warfare" (Book 2, 17) and "They kill, they cut in pieces" (Book 8, 51)—but no prolonged reflection or detailed description. As for the plague, Marcus makes just a single direct reference, comparing falsehoods to plague: both are toxic, both are to be avoided. Remarkably, though, the former is more poisonous. "For corruption of the mind is a far graver pestilence than any comparable disturbance and alteration in the air that surrounds us; for the one is a plague to living creatures as mere animals, and the other to human beings in their nature as human beings."

When I first read this passage, I thought it must be a rhetorical lapse. For the last ten years of his reign, Marcus had struggled with the unprecedented economic and demographic consequences of the plague. He must have seen, like his personal doctor Galen, the horrifying impact of the disease on the body; the inner citadel he had built must have been rocked to its very foundations by this pestilence. How, then, could he possibly have believed that lies are worse than *loimoi*, or plagues?

But I was wrong. Marcus sincerely—and consistently—believed that false perceptions are more deadly than real diseases. For a Stoic, denying what our eyes and minds convey prevents our acting in accord with the world. It blinds us not only to what needs to be done, but also to what attaches us to others: a shared humanity based on the faculty of reason. Those who fail to see and speak clearly about the nature of things, Marcus reminds himself, are lost souls. What should we think, he concludes, "about the man who fears or courts the applause of an audience who have no idea where they are or who they are?" The question is no less urgent today than it was two millennia ago.

This allergy to falsehoods, this insistence on seeing and describing things as they truly are, has consequences. It transforms, for example, our attitude toward death. Thanks to his Stoic apprenticeship, Marcus had faced death long before he faced war and plague. By always rehearsing for the end of life—a role that could be thrust upon him at any moment—he sought to rid himself of the fear of death. His guide Epictetus found many ways to convey the same truth: though we have no power over the time and nature of our death, we do have power over our attitude toward it. By reminding ourselves, through various techniques, of death, death will lose its hold on us. We must constantly remind ourselves that our selves are liable to be extinguished at any moment. "Let death and exile," Epictetus exhorted, "be daily before your eyes, but death chiefly; and you will never entertain any abject thought, nor too eagerly covet anything." In an echo of Epictetus, Marcus reminds himself: "You may leave this life at any moment: have this possibility in your mind in all that you do or say or think" (Book 2, 11).

In effect, Marcus strives to reach a "view from above" (Book 9, 30) in regard to death. By pulling away from his own death and pulling toward a perspective that casts that death as the dimmest of flickers in the cosmic lightshow, Marcus no longer takes death personally. Among his many entries on death, Marcus often quotes Epictetus, reminding himself that he is "a soul carrying a corpse" (Book 4, 41) and that death "is a relief from the reaction to the senses, from the puppet strings of impulse, from the analytical mind, and from service to the flesh" (Book 6, 28). He casts his eye across the past, noting how those feared or praised during their lives—the Caesars and sages—are no more, just as he will soon be no more.

Indeed, he reminds himself to take nothing personally. Everything that falls outside the inner fortress of reason and is beyond our control are things indifferent. What we can control, once again, is our attitude and actions toward them. We must, in turn, master this control by constant reminder and continuous practice. It requires sustained vigilance, but also sustained abstraction. The view from above is a view that abstracts; from this height, the individuals with whom we live, each endowed with a unique past and personality, tend to congeal into a concept. The entirety of humanity becomes one's purview, and the *kosmopolitai*—the universal city-state of reasoning citizens—becomes one's home. While we might give more attention to our child or parent, that is not because they hold greater value, but simply because they live in closer proximity. The cosmopolitan view from above dictates that we must not give special attention to any one individual or group of individuals, but instead treat all human beings with the same attention. Indeed, the intrinsic worth we normally give to those human beings near and dear—that bonds like love and friendship make our lives worthwhile—succeeds only in making us captives of fortune. We must avoid feeling compassion for others because it attaches us to things indifferent and beyond our control. It is a passion—a surge of the irrational within us—that we must not embrace, but instead extirpate. By all means help someone grieving for a loss, Marcus reminds himself, "but do not imagine their loss as any real harm—that is the wrong way of thinking" (Book 5, 36).

"I have been plainly told," Cassius Dio writes in his history, that Marcus Aurelius's doctors, "at the behest of Commodus, provoked the emperor's death in 180 CE." If this is true, Commudus's act is unforgivable. But if Marcus were a true Stoic sage, he might find that his son's act, while unforgivable, is perhaps understandable.

...

When I first met Mr. R, he was curled up on his bed and cocooned in several blankets. Holding a food tray by his bed in the darkened room, I whispered, "Mr. R?" A muffled "Yes?" rose from the bundle of linen. I looked for his face, but along with the rest of his body, it was hidden. Trying to sound perky while still whispering, I said: "I brought your five-star dinner." "Please leave it on the table," the voice replied. "I'll get to it later." Uncertain what to do, I did as Mr. R asked and tiptoed out of the room. As I reached the door, the voice added: "Thank you." When I returned an hour later to pick up the tray, I found that it was untouched.

This, I discovered, was the rule with Mr. R. His treating physical therapist told me that Mr. R was debilitated not just by cancer, but also by depression. Unlike many other residents, though, his mind was not at all debilitated. This is what made his case so daunting for those committed to making him healthier: Mr. R did not share the same commitment and lucidly explained why. On several occasions, he told the therapist that he didn't want to recover his upper-body strength. Instead, he wanted to die. At times, Mr. R would allow the therapist to put him in a wheelchair and take him to the rehab gym, where he would politely go through the motions for forty-five minutes. Once back in his room, however, he would return to bed and burrow under the blankets. To keep Mr. R away from his bed—away from his self, really—the therapist, taking time from her own schedule, began to take him outside, to an inner patio sheltered from the plague-beleaguered world beyond the residence, where they would sit and chat.

Inspired by her example, I began to do the same with Mr. R. While I looked at his face—the cheeks gaunt, skin discolored, eyes grayish blue, and teeth deep yellow—Mr. R told me tales of his days in the "military" and "industry." He never explained which branch of the military or what kind of industry, but it did not really matter since both were wrapped in mystery. Pulling at his face mask, he explained that his task was to keep an eye on the local population. More mysteriously, he remarked that he was sent to other countries to make certain that what his superiors expected was what in fact occurred. I would nod my head and express my wonder, all the while asking myself if he was a fabulist. Or, instead, a dying man glad to have the unexpected chance, in a nursing home that he knew would be his last home, to explain himself to a historian.

Of course, as the Stoics remind us, we are dying the moment we are born. But Mr. R would have little truck with such mental tonics: his death was present, looming as heavily as the tree shadows did in the courtyard. He was perfectly aware of this—he was, I believe, the most clear-minded resident at the home—and seemed perfectly unperturbed. One afternoon, after a long pause in our conversation, Mr. R said, "I've lived my life. I would like to die." I didn't know what to say and, suddenly ill at ease, I stood up. Gripping the back of the wheelchair, I blurted, "I'm sure your children wouldn't agree with you" and wheeled him back to his room. To be honest, I did not have the slightest idea what his children would have thought.

In mid-June, a few weeks after I left the residence, the therapist contacted me: Mr. R, who had been put on hospice care, had died the night before. I was stunned by the news and was utterly unable to think of Mr. R's life and death as something indifferent. The message of the *Meditations* suddenly seemed as distant as ancient Rome. But I then recalled a passage where Marcus seemed to address this very moment. In Book 5, he writes that when the mind fails before the body, the latter becomes rudderless. For this reason, it is for the helmsman to decide when the moment has come to dock. "You can live here in this world just as you intend to live when you have left it. But if this is not allowed you, then you should depart life itself—but not as if there were some misfortune. 'The fire smokes and I leave the house.' Why think this any big matter? But as long as no such thing drives me out, I remain a free man and no one will prevent me doing what I wish to do: and my wish is to follow the nature of a rational and social being" (Book 5, 29).

3

MICHEL DE MONTAIGNE AND THE BUBONIC PLAGUE

He was not a hero and never pretended to be. STEFAN ZWEIG

Our duty is to compose our character, not to compose books.
MICHEL DE MONTAIGNE

In June 1585, Michel de Montaigne was cleaning up his affairs as the mayor of Bordeaux. He was nearly at the end of his second two-year term, and all that remained was for him to hand over the city keys to his successor. But Montaigne was also, quite literally, trying to clean up: his city of 40,000—the fifth largest in France—was a sorry pigsty. Despite several official warnings, the residents continued to strew trash on the city streets. As this was Bordeaux, the littering included buckets of cod and herring remains, heaved from windows onto the streets and pedestrians below. It was urgent, the mayor's office announced, to prevent "the infection and stench of sewage, manure, refuse, and other filth."[1] It was not the mayor's first health ordonnance—he had ordered, one year earlier, the twice-weekly collection of refuse—but it proved to be the last.

In late June, the bubonic plague burst upon Bordeaux. The

region's governor, Maréchal de Matignon, described the consequences in a letter to King Henry III: "The plague is spreading so quickly in this city that no one remains who has the means to flee."[2] While municipal authorities struggled to maintain order, the city's parliamentarians joined the exodus. They decamped to Libourne, a nearby town that served as a refuge for well-to-do Bordelais ever since the black rat, the carrier of the plague bacillus, first disembarked onto French soil in the fourteenth century. As for the city's poor, their grim fate was sealed: by year's end, between 14,000 and 16,000 men, women, and children—nearly one-half of Bordeaux's population—had contracted the disease and died inside the city walls.[3]

Truth be told, Montaigne was not inside those same walls. The pestilential storm that had broken over the city found him at his nearby ancestral chateau, spending the final days of his second and last term of office. Plans had already been made for Montaigne to attend the ceremony on August 1 for the formal transition of power to Matignon. When he learned of the plague, his peers had already fled the city. As for the poor, the situation was dismal. In a letter to Montaigne on July 30, Matignon declared that commoners—*le menu people*—were "dying like flies."[4] What was Montaigne to do? He had just two days left in his term of office, while Matignon, his successor, was already at his post in the city. If he were to enter Bordeaux, what could he possibly do during those forty-eight hours to help the city? Would not his own death, on the eve of his retirement, be a hollow heroic gesture? Yet one more burden to place on the overwhelmed authorities, yet one more body to be carted and buried in a mass grave?

Astride his horse, Montaigne left his chateau and approached Bordeaux, stopping at Libourne. From there, he sent a letter to the municipal *jurats*, promising to obey a command he hoped they would not issue. Declaring that he would "spare neither my life nor anything else," Montaigne quickly explained why such a sacrifice was worse than useless. "I will leave you to judge whether the service I can render you by my presence at the coming election is worth risking going into the city in view of the bad condition it is in."[5] He sent a second letter the following day, once again asking what was expected of him. As there is no record of a reply, we do not know if the *jurats* replied to the letters or, for that matter, were still around to do so. In any case, when the day of the official ceremony came and went, Montaigne turned his horse around and returned to his chateau.

...

Bubonic plagues were to coastal regions in early modern France what hurricanes are to coastal regions in postmodern America: catastrophic and common. From the mid-fourteenth to mid-seventeenth centuries, nearly fifty pestilential storms struck France, mostly along the country's Atlantic and Mediterranean flanks.[6] Yet the comparison goes only so far. Hurricanes come and go, while plagues come and stay; hurricanes wreak havoc on buildings and infrastructure, while plagues wreak havoc on the human body and body politic. It is for this reason that the bubonic plague inspires a dread and captures our imagination in a way that even the most disastrous hurricanes cannot.

Beyond reporting that people were "dying like flies," Matignon does not bother to detail the plague's impact on its victims. Given the official nature of the letter, but also the well-known nature of the plague, there was no need to. Had Matignon thought to send a description, however, it would not have differed greatly from the description offered by a resident of Marseilles of the plague that swept through his city in 1720. "All we see are people collapsing in the streets, stricken by sudden death, or others on the point of death who, dragging themselves along, are ready to quit life at the first turn in the street. There are others who, having escaped from their beds, run in a frenzy through the streets, spreading the invisible traits of the fatal disease. Corpses are piled on top of one another, often half-decomposed, dragged to burial pits by family members who are terrified to meet the same sad fate striking down so many others."[7]

Nor would Matignon's description have differed dramatically from accounts of the Black Death that, beginning in the mid-fourteenth century, ravaged France and the rest of Europe. In his provocative claim that French history was essentially "motionless"—*une histoire immobile*—from the 1300s to 1800s, Emmanuel Le Roy Ladurie emphasizes that the country's population remained static during that period, hovering between 15 and 17 million inhabitants. A major reason for zero population growth, he suggests, was the Black Death and cortege of other epidemics that crisscrossed the country. A consequence of the burgeoning of maritime exploration of new lands and brutal subjugation of their populations, these epidemics included syphilis and typhus.[8] Yet the ferocity of the bubonic plague, which exploded in buboes on the victim's body, was the most dreadful. With a snap of its fingers, *la morte noire* halved Bordeaux's population of 30,000 during the second half of the fourteenth century.

…

Death was no stranger to Montaigne. Not only had five of his six daughters died in infancy—he and his wife had no sons—but Montaigne was long afflicted by life-threatening kidney stones. Moreover, in 1569 he had a near-death experience on his property. Thrown off his horse in a violent collision with another rider, Montaigne, splayed motionless on the ground, appeared dead to his entourage. Carried back to his chateau, he recovered the next day—no doubt helped by refusing the many medical remedies he was offered—yet suffered from the shock for several years. It seemed, he later recalled, that "my life was hanging only by the tip of my lips; I closed my eyes in order, it seemed to me, to help push it out, and took pleasure in growing languid and letting myself go."[9]

Most famously, there was the death of his friend Etienne de La Boétie. When the recently appointed Montaigne had first met La Boétie at the Bordeaux Parlement in 1559, the slightly older La Boétie was already an influential magistrate, as well as author of *On Voluntary Servitude*. In a gripping exploration of the relationship between tyrants and tyrannized, La Boétie dwells on the alchemy that occurs when suppression begets not just submission, but sycophancy. "What strange phenomenon is this?" he exclaims. "What name shall we give to it? What is the nature of this misfortune? What vice is it, or, rather, what degradation? To see an endless multitude of people not merely obeying but driven to servility?"[10] They surrender to servility, in part, because of the spectacles offered by tyrants. With such enticements, La Boétie writes, "stupefied peoples, fascinated by the pastimes and vain pleasures flashed before their eyes, learned subservience." Moreover, they accept the yoke of oppression because they believe that because it has always been thus and remains thus, it was meant to be always thus. In this fashion, they "invest those who order them around with proprietary rights, based on the idea that it has always been that way." Finally, in an uncanny anticipation of Max Weber's analysis of charisma—a power dynamic that depends as much on the ruled as the ruler—La Boétie suggests that the tyrannized attribute to the tyrant the very qualities that seduce them.

Fortunately, there are exceptions to this dismal rule. There are, La Boétie declares, a happy few whose character and education immunize them to the attractions of servitude. Such is the natural bent of their minds, that even "if liberty had entirely perished from the earth, such men would invent it. For them slavery has no satisfactions, no matter how well disguised." These men, La Boétie believes, are immune to the deep and abiding human desire to surrender our freedom to a powerful figure. It is to this band of exceptional men, able to resist the hold tyrants exercise on their subjects, that La Boétie aims his treatise. But in case they have forgotten who they are and of what they are capable, La Boétie gives them a good shaking: "Resolve no longer to be slaves and you are free!"

Yet La Boétie was also resolved to leave his treatise unpublished. To have the work printed during the reign of the young and unstable Charles IX would have amounted to an act of self-immolation. And so, La Boétie muted his clarion call, restricting the treatise to circulate in manuscript form among his peers. Nevertheless, the work left an enduring mark on the young and impressionable Montaigne. Struck by the independence but also prudence of La Boétie, Montaigne described La Boétie's mind as one "molded in the pattern of other ages than this."[11] Not surprisingly, once the two men met in Bordeaux, they became fast friends. Indeed, it was a friendship in which the two became one, a blending of souls so complete as to "efface the seam that joined them." We found ourselves, Montaigne later recalled—or, perhaps, recreated—"so taken with each other, so well acquainted, so bound together, that from that time on nothing was so close to us as each other."[12]

The friendship, however, lasted scarcely four years. In 1563, La Boétie, not yet thirty-three, died after a protracted illness. The nature of the disease is not clear—La Boétie was stricken by bloody diarrhea and a high fever—but both he and Montaigne diagnosed it as the plague. Whatever its nature, it proved fatal. With her husband bed-ridden and weakening, Madame de La Boétie sent a letter to Montaigne, warning him of his friend's imminent demise. Hastening to Bordeaux, Montaigne remained at La Boétie's bedside until his death a week later.

Yet Montaigne was not alone at the bedside. It was a crowded affair, teeming with family, friends, and colleagues. Such crowds—in effect, audiences—were then common. As the historian Philippe Ariès suggests, the sixteenth century belonged to the "age of tame death."[13] By this, Ariès means an age when death was both a familiar and public rite of passage. It was that pivotal moment of life when the dying were called upon to direct their death. It was a staged piece replete with a script, one that girded the dying individual for his own passing and, through edifying words, guided those being left behind. It was a ritual that included the making of speeches and offering of exhortations to live good and Christian lives. La Boétie was no exception. He did make many speeches—transcribed by Montaigne, who quietly noted that they "were a little long"—and called upon his family to cherish his memory.[14] In his last words to Montaigne, still sitting by his bed, La Boétie sighed, "For three days now I have been straining to leave."[15]

...

I had never seen the body of someone who, straining to leave their body, finally succeeded. At least until the moment I walked into Mrs. W's room. Carrying her food tray, I saw her skeletal body, showered in the sunlight streaming through the window, spread across her bed. Her eyes were closed, but I didn't think it was sleep. Her mouth was twisted into a grimace, but I knew, or so I thought, that this time it was not because she hated the food. Her pale blue gown, one corner sagging below a wilted breast, looked like a death shroud.

Setting the tray on her bedside table, I leaned over her body and gingerly raised her drooping gown top. Her chest seemed motionless. I called her name once, then twice in a soft, strangled voice. Suddenly, I asked myself why I was whispering. There was no one else in the room—the other bed, stripped bare, was unoccupied—and, well, Mrs. W was dead. My earlier visits to her room usually ended in retreat, as she flailed her thin arms and flung insults at me. It was odd to see her now so silent, still, but in death as in life, clearly not at peace. Uncertain what to do, I tiptoed out of the room to find a nurse or aide—anyone, really—to whom I could report the news. The first person I glimpsed down the hall was A., the always smiling, always chatting activities director. This position, I confusedly thought, made A. more qualified than a nurse for this moment. Catching her eye, I motioned for her to follow me to the room. At the door, I whispered—again—that I thought something was wrong with Mrs. W. When A. asked why, I replied, "I think she's dead."

Thankfully, she did not then ask why I was whispering. Instead, looking first at me, then at Mrs. W, A. realized she was not the best person for the situation. Hurrying down the hall to find a nurse, she returned a few minutes later with R., the director of nursing and the sort of petite yet powerful Texan you (barely) see behind the wheel of a Chevy Suburban negotiating the speed bumps in mall parking lots. With a soft Texas twang, R. addressed everyone, from her children to the director, as "Ma'am" or "Sir." Never sure if it was meant to suggest respect or menace, I mostly kept my distance, as I did when she and A. entered the room.

Resisting the urge to rubberneck, I returned to the food cart at the end of the hall. About fifteen minutes later, as I was leaving a room juggling two food-spattered and ice-tea-soaked trays, R. stopped in front of me. "I've something to show you," she said. Following her back to Mrs. W's room, R. pointed toward the deceased occupant. Her eyes were still closed and the food tray, untouched, sat in front of her. Seeing my puzzled expression, R. walked over to the bed and bent toward Mrs. W: "Ma'am, can I help you with your dinner?" Her eyes suddenly opening, she roared, "No, I don't want your help and don't want your food!" As shouts exploded across the room, R. and I retreated to the hallway. Turning to me with a triumphant look, she declared, "You see, Mrs. W was just being her old self." She then returned to the nurses' station while I returned to the cart.

When I arrived at the residence the following afternoon, I followed the usual routine: washing my hands at the outdoor sink, checking the same boxes on the health questionnaire, and having my temperature taken by the admissions director (who, for obvious reasons, had little else to do). As I headed to the kitchen, A. hurried up to me. Grabbing my arm with a gloved hand and trying to hold back tears, she told me that Mrs. W had died that morning. Dazed, I nodded my head and thanked her for telling me. I was not surprised, to be honest, but I was shocked. The day before, when I had brought by her food tray, I think I glimpsed her effort to leave. Rather than sit by her bed, I fled the room, appalled by the prospect of being in the same room with death. And now I am appalled to realize that, while believing I was playing a minor role in the taming of Mrs. W's death, instead I played a role in the wilding of her final hours.

...

What Montaigne described as a "plague of the utmost severity" soon spilled over the walls of Bordeaux and reached the walls of his chateau. At that moment, he later wrote, "I confronted an absurd situation: the sight of my house was frightful to me." Feverishly packing the essentials, including his manuscript of his collected essays, Montaigne herded his elderly mother, wife, and daughter into a carriage and quit their estate. "All that was in it was unguarded and abandoned to anyone who wanted it."[16] From one day to the next, Montaigne and his family had become exiles, alienated not just from their home, but also from their former selves, selves that were defined by daily routines and rituals, expectations and aspirations.

Once on the road with his family, Montaigne found that it was as impossible to escape the plague's shadow. Wherever he and his family went, they "spread horror" as possible carriers of the infection. Forced "to change their abode as soon as any one of them began to feel so much as an ache in one fingertip," those fleeing the plague came to fear their own selves as much as others feared them. And for good reason: "As for the people round about, not a hundredth could save themselves." The pestilence's ubiquity infected with terrifying portents the most commonplace of experiences or encounters. The contagion assaulted not just the body, but also the mind. "After any approach to danger you have to be forty days in a trance of anxiety over that illness, with your imagination meanwhile working you up in its own way and turning even your health into a fever."[17]

The verdant fields and vineyards of the Gironde were now littered with the dead and dying. Those who had cultivated the land now threw themselves into pits they themselves had dug. While the "grapes remained hanging on the vines," the peasants submitted to their fates, waiting for "death that evening or the next day." From the road, Montaigne passed scene after nightmarish scene. He saw peasants lying dead in the fields, prey to wolves or dogs that "promptly appeared in swarms." He saw one of his own workers "with his hands and feet pull the earth over him as he was dying."[18] How should *we* see Montaigne at these moments? Did he speak or gesture to the man? Did he turn away? Indeed, what could he have said or done? For "six months of misery," Montaigne guided his anxious and alarmed caravan of family and retainers from place to place. When he returned to his chateau the following year, he returned something of a changed man—a change registered by the peculiar instrument with which he spent the preceding decade measuring and molding himself: *Les Essais*.

...

Retirement is the moment, for many, to try—*assay*, *essay*—new skills, new interests, new pursuits. For Montaigne, it was a case of essaying what was as old as he himself—indeed, his very self. In 1571, the thirty-something nobleman quit the Parlement of Bordeaux, where he had served for more than a decade as a magistrate. Even for the sixteenth century, little more than ten years in a job and little less than forty years of a life do not seem long enough to warrant retirement. Nevertheless, Montaigne decided the time was right to swap a life of parliamentary palaver for a life of philosophical pondering. By way of daily exhortation, he had a Latin inscription painted on the wall outside his library: "Michel de Montaigne, long weary of the servitude of the court and public employments, while still entire, retired to the bosom of the Muses where in calm and freedom from all cares he will spend what little remains of his life now more than half run out." (It was not, of course, unusual for French aristocrats to cite Latin phrases. But Montaigne's fluency was unusual: thanks to the zealous humanism of his father, he spoke and heard only Latin until the age of six.)

Yet he found his new life of idleness even more full of cares than his old life of activity. Melancholy overtook Montaigne as a life of leisure was lurching into a life of lassitude. His mind, freed from dreary external obligations, had been captured by violent internal oscillations. "Unless you keep it busy with some definite subject that will bridle and control it, it throws itself in disorder hither and yon in the vague field of imagination." His disordered mind, which he compared to a "runaway horse," now gave birth to "so many chimeras and fantastic monsters, one after another, without order or purpose." Determined to bridle his inner tumult, Montaigne decided to "put them in writing, hoping in time to make my mind ashamed of itself."[19] In an essay he began a few years later, "Of the Affection of Fathers for Their Children," Montaigne returns to the origins of what he calls "the only book of its kind in the world." He began to write, he reflects, during "the gloom of the solitude into which I had cast myself some years ago." Finding himself "destitute and void of any other matter, I presented myself to myself for argument and subject."[20]

Given the "wild and eccentric plan" for this undertaking, Montaigne at first tethered his writings to quotations from ancient Greek and Roman philosophers and poets, historians and tragedians. Despite the image we might have of Montaigne seated at his desk, reading the ancients and jotting down his reflections, he instead would pace across the oaken floor of the library, picking up and putting down books, while dictating to his secretary. Initially, quotations were copious, the commentaries were curt, and the organization was casual. The initial batch of essays were like balls of sourdough to which Montaigne, occasionally kneading, kept adding new material.

By 1580, Montaigne had "baked" a grand total of ninety-four essays, with fifty-seven packaged into a Book 1 and thirty-seven more into a Book 2. While their titles suggested that they treated specific topics—virtues like friendship and moderation, vices such as idleness and vanity, and emotions like solitude and fear—the essays often rambled across several topics in the space of a single page. "I leaf through one book, now another, without order and without plan, by disconnected fragments," he explained. "One moment I muse, another moment I set down or dictate, walking back and forth, these fancies of mine that you see here."[21]

A great admirer of Montaigne, the eighteenth-century philosopher Denis Diderot, famously declared, through a fictional alter-ego in his dizzying dialogue *Rameau's Nephew*, that ideas are his trollops. Wherever they lead, he gladly follows. This is also true for Montaigne, but it is even truer for his reveries and reflections, sensations and sentiments. His entire being, mind and body, is the subject of his essays, yet, as he observes, he "cannot keep my subject still. It goes along befuddled and staggering, with a natural drunkenness. I do not portray being; I portray passing. Not the passing from one age to another . . . but from day to day, minute to minute."[22] Montaigne goes one step further than Heraclitus: not only can he not put his foot in the same river twice, but he cannot do so even once. Between the moment his skin touches water and the moment his brain registers the contact, everything has changed.

In such a situation, what can one do? The answer turns out to be essaying. If his mind could "find a firm footing," Montaigne announces, he would not need to write essays. Instead, he "would make decisions." But as it stands, neither the world nor his self stands still long enough to make an enduring decision. From the moment of our birth, we are swallowed into phenomenological riot, a sea of constant change on which we are not an island but instead a cork. As a result, the act of essaying is less an attempt at casting anchor or finding a mooring than it is a never-ending series of trials, or *essais*, at capturing the moment—at capturing oneself—as it passes from being into having been. It seems as if writers have been essaying their stream of consciousness ever since William James coined the phrase in the late nineteenth century. Yet, five hundred years earlier, Montaigne had the audacity to declare: "I study myself more than any other subject. That is my metaphysics, that is my physics."[23] By clambering onto the essay form, a literary raft largely of his own making, Montaigne was the first to strike out on the whitewater of inner sensations.

While riding these cascades, death was Montaigne's constant companion. Not death as the possible outcome of a collision with a boulder or bank, but instead death as the only outcome of each and every life. Montaigne's early preoccupation with death was not morbid, but Stoic. As we saw with Marcus Aurelius, Stoicism sought to change not just one's ideas, but one's very self. Stoic sages like Epictetus urged their students to distinguish between things external and internal, things we can and things we cannot control. By making this claim our own, we can free ourselves from the vicissitudes of life. Montaigne takes up this perspective in an early essay, aptly titled "That the Taste of Good and Evil Depends in Large Part on the Opinion We Have of Them." Fortune neither helps nor harms us, he declares. Instead, it only offers us the material for good or evil which "our soul, more powerful than fortune, turns and applies as it pleases, sole cause and mistress of its happy or unhappy condition."[24]

For the Stoic, then, the tool for living is thus a tool for dying—a tool eagerly taken up by Montaigne in the earlier essays. The title to one essay paraphrases Seneca's famous declaration: To philosophize is to learn how to die. In effect, Montaigne assays the ways to strip death "of its strangeness." Never underestimate death's capacity to surprise us; never overestimate our capacity to believe we are exempt. Though we always avert our eyes from death, it always stalks us. Rather than treating it as we would an uninvited guest, Montaigne advises, we should instead acknowledge it. Since we are "uncertain where death awaits us, let us await it everywhere. Premeditation of death is premeditation of freedom. He who has learned how to die has unlearned how to be a slave."[25] For this reason, death must always be front and center in our thoughts. Especially when we are enjoying our lives, "let us keep in mind the memory of our condition . . . and that our happiness is prey to death." Turning to the Stoic sages to steel himself for the unpredictable yet inevitable arrival of death, Montaigne thus yokes his life to the thought of death: "The goal of our career is death. It is the necessary object of our aim."[26]

...

Even if Montaigne were not interested in death, death was interested in him. A year before witnessing the death of his friend La Boétie, he witnessed what appeared to be the imminent death of his country. On March 1, 1562, armed Catholic extremists set upon several hundred Huguenots—the name for French Protestants—who were illegally praying in a barn in Vassy, a town in the Champagne region. In the ensuing massacre, dozens of Huguenots were killed, and more than a hundred maimed. For a country where religious divisions between Catholics and Protestants had festered for decades, the consequences were clear. Upon hearing the news of the massacre, Montaigne's friend, the Parisian lawyer Etienne Pasquier, wrote, "All one talks about now is war . . . and there is nothing to be more feared in a state than civil war . . . If it was permitted to me to assess these events, I would tell you that it was the beginning of a tragedy."[27]

Tragedy is not the only word to describe the several decades of religious and civil warfare that followed the events at Vassy.

Fear and loathing—the sentiments Catholics and Huguenots felt for one another in sixteenth-century France—are other words that do just as well. The mutual distrust and detestation felt by both camps explains why, between 1562 and 1598, they fought eight distinct and separate wars—wars in which each side, equally convinced that they had God's blessing, made little distinction between civilians and soldiers. Among the war's first casualties was the fragile distinction between combat and butchery. The basso continuo of violence became a constant in the lives of the French, regardless of the side they had chosen—or, indeed, refused to choose. As Montaigne observed toward the end of his life, "In this confusion that we have been in for thirty years every Frenchman, whether as an individual or as a member of the community, sees himself at every moment on the verge of the total overthrow of his fortune."[28]

Rarely have the depths of misfortune been more fully plumbed than on August 24, 1572: Saint Bartholomew's Day. Early that morning, the woeful Charles IX and his forceful mother, Catherine de Medici, ordered the assassination of the leaders of the Protestant community, gathered in Paris for the marriage of the Protestant Henri of Navarre and the Catholic Marguerite de Valois. What was meant to be a surgical strike against a few dozen commanders, however, billowed into a bloodbath that stretched over several days. Whipped into a frenzy by Catholic preachers calling upon them to do God's work, persuaded the Huguenots were an existential threat, Catholics murdered at least 2,000 of their Protestant neighbors. The Seine turned red from the hundreds of mutilated bodies it carried downstream, while other bodies were burned or left to the dogs. The crowd's cruelty simply defies description. To give but one example, several Catholics burst into the house of the Huguenot artisan Philippe Le Doux, in bed with his wife, who was pregnant with their twenty-first child. The marauders instantly killed the husband, while the wife, who asked to first be allowed to give birth, tried to escape when the killers rejected her request. They sliced open her abdomen, exposed the unborn child, and threw both bodies into the street.[29]

Bordeaux and the surrounding region proved especially vulnerable to the virus of religious hatred, infecting local Protestants as well as Catholics. In retaliation for the assassination in 1569 of their leader, the Duc de Condé, Huguenots massacred hundreds of Catholic peasants in the region. Three years later, it was the turn of the Catholics. The madness unleashed in Paris on Saint Bartholomew's Day surged across the country and reached as far as Bordeaux. Worried that calls by local Catholic priests to emulate their Parisian brethren would lead to the same uncontrolled torrent of violence, officials tried to contain popular passion by preempting it. They ordered the execution of 250 Protestants, including members of the Parlement, in early October. Cloistered at his chateau, Montaigne never commented, at least publicly, during these events. As Philippe Desan observes, prudence was then a matter of life or death: "Montaigne had several friends who had made the mistake of committing themselves too much to one camp or the other."[30] As with his decision not to enter plague-ridden Bordeaux, Montaigne's silence will disappoint those readers in search of heroes—unless, that is, they revise their understanding of heroism.

...

Casual readers of the *Essays* probably do not know that, until the horrific events of Saint Bartholomew's Day, Montaigne largely sided with the Catholics. Paradoxically, though, he did so not as a true believer but instead as a true doubter. In a word, as a Skeptic. Not the sort, however, who through laziness or apathy never commits to a cause or principle. Instead, it was the sort of Skepticism attained through serious and systematic reasoning that leads to a suspension of judgment.

In particular, Montaigne was fascinated by Pyrrhonian Skepticism, a particular approach named after the third century BCE thinker Pyrrho and systematized by Sextus Empiricus a few centuries later. Not unlike a postmodern relativist, the Pyrrhonian Skeptic dismissed the possibility of discovering universal and eternal truths. In his treatise, Sextus sets out to show that for every proposition, an opposing claim can be formulated. This undermines not just reason's ability to settle on a single position, but also the desirability of trying to do so. As the wars of religion made all too clear, to stake out a particular belief was a source not just of great personal anxiety, but also of great social discord. For this reason, when faced with competing truth claims, the Skeptic declares a pox on both sides and refuses to choose.[31] Rather than Jean-Paul Sartre's claim, two millennia later, that not to choose is the worst of all choices, the Skeptic suggests that it is the best of choices a person can make.

By way of advertising his Skeptic credentials, Montaigne had the Greek word *Epokhe* chiseled into a ceiling beam of his library and engraved on a medallion. As he explains in his longest essay, "An Apology for Raymond Sebond," it means "I hold back, I do not budge."[32] Practicing Skeptics—not at all the same creature as an academic skeptic—thus abstain from absolutes and refrain from resolutions. Instead, they "use their reason to inquire and debate, but not to conclude and choose. Whoever will imagine a perpetual confession of ignorance, a judgment without leaning or inclination, on any occasion whatever, he has a conception of Pyrrhonism."[33]

What better occasion to practice Pyrrhonism than in the

midst of a religious bloodletting driven by fanatics on both sides? Given the ultimately unverifiable truth claims made by both Catholics and Protestants, Montaigne reasoned, his reason left him no choice but to suspend judgment. Skepticism struck him as the most reasonable of stances. In an early essay, "Of Freedom of Conscience," Montaigne asserts that "good intentions, if they are carried out without moderation, push men to very vicious acts." Since the ultimate validity of any claim cannot be ascertained, it makes the most sense to stick with the tried and true. For this reason, "In this controversy on whose account France is agitated by civil wars, the best and soundest side is undoubtedly that which maintains both the old religion and the old government of the country."[34]

In essence, it is a brand of conservatism marked not by positive claims, but instead by enlightened convenience. Like La Boétie, Montaigne made a hard-and-fast distinction between public and private selves. While the latter thrives on the free rein of thought, the former requires its suspension. The sage, he insisted, "should withdraw his soul within, out of the crowd, and keep it in freedom and power to judge things freely; but as for externals, he should wholly follow the accepted fashions and forms. Society in general can do without our thoughts; but the rest—our actions, our work, our fortunes and our very life—we must lend and abandon to its service and to common opinions."[35]

But Montaigne's embrace of the old religion and old government faltered in the aftermath of the Saint Bartholomew's Day Massacre. The recently retired Montaigne now began to distance himself from not just the Catholic cause but any cause capable of fueling such acts. Was it not extraordinary to cut throats over, say, the recondite matter of transubstantiation versus consubstantiation? In his essay "Of Cannibals," written after he met a group of Tupinambá natives from Brazil who had been brought to Rouen in 1550, he observes that barbarism is in the eyes of the beholder. "I am not sorry that we notice the barbarous horror of such acts, but I am heartily sorry that, judging their faults rightly, we should be so blind to our own." Indeed, Montaigne continues, "we might call these barbarians in respect to the rules of reason, but not in respect to ourselves, who surpass them in every kind of barbarity."[36]

Montaigne concludes his essay with a famous flourish. Upon reporting a couple of enlightened replies to questions he asked a Tupinambá native—he had actually asked three questions, but remarks, with typical candor, that he has forgotten the third one—Montaigne observes: "All this is not too bad—but what's the use? They don't wear breeches." When we look up from the page—when *I* look up from the page—we savor both the obvious irony and our own exceptionality. Those sixteenth-century French, we tell ourselves, just did not get it. Secure in their traditional beliefs and values, they dismissed the Tupinambá as barbarians while believing themselves to be paragons of civilization. And they did so despite wearing splendid breeches stained in the blood of their fellow men and women. Nodding our heads at our copies of the *Essays*, we also tell ourselves how many of our own contemporaries do not get it, either. Secure in their traditional news silos or virtual communities, they deny the humanity of those from other silos and other communities, real or virtual. But we, of course, think we get it—or, at least, I think that *I*, at least, get it.

Except that I don't. Consider the case of that great artist of irony, Socrates, who also happened to be Montaigne's hero. Readers of the Platonic dialogues relish the skill with which Socrates employs irony against interlocutors who are as fatuous as they are firm in their beliefs. Time and again, Socrates maneuvers them into logical impasses, dazed and often angry to find they cannot defend a proposition or principle they had always believed to be true. We first nod our heads at their discomfort, then shake our heads at their dimness, and finish with a self-satisfied laugh. Though their claim has been exploded, these benighted souls nevertheless return to their lives they had lived before meeting Socrates, neither changing how they live nor how they think.

But, as the philosopher Alexander Nehamas suggests, the real object of Socratic irony is not the dialogue's interlocutor, but the dialogue's reader. Just as Socrates's victim picks up where he left off, so do we. Socrates is right, we tell ourselves, and his interlocutor is wrong, but we almost always fail to extend this investigation to our own selves. We refuse to examine our own beliefs and certitudes, and adjust our lives accordingly, with the same clarity and determination that Socrates brings to his contemporaries and his own self. As a result, we are, Nehamas writes, "simply displaying our ignorance of our own ignorance. In the process of producing in us a disdain for Socrates' interlocutors, the dialogues turn us into characters just like them."[37]

Having spent the last decades of his life studying that same life, Montaigne understood a thing or two about Socratic irony. He had been wrong too many times about things he felt certain to be foolish to trust his judgment again. But that is just the first step. "To learn that we have said or done a foolish thing, that is nothing; we must learn that we are nothing but fools, a far broader and more important lesson." And a lesson, of course, so much more difficult to act upon. It is no easy matter to act on the insight that what we most often lack is self-insight, whether taught by a Socratic dialogue or a Montaignian essay. To change an idea requires great effort; to change a life conforming to that changed idea demands nearly superhuman exertion. While I am not wearing breeches—wrong century, wrong season, wrong city—it seems, even now as I write, that I might as well be.

...

"He was not a hero and he never pretended to be." With a typically lapidary phrase, Stefan Zweig—a man who did wear breeches, and very stylish breeches at that—thus described Montaigne's response to the plague.[38] In late 1941, the cosmopolitan and cultivated Austrian writer was, all too improbably, living in the Brazilian town of Petrópolis with his wife, Lotte. No less improbably, he had found an old copy of Montaigne's essays in the cellar of the house they were renting. As he wrote to his friend, the French novelist Jules Romains, he glommed on to Montaigne "like a discovery." Certain authors, he explained, "reveal themselves to us only at a certain age and in chosen moments."[39] Sitting on his tropical veranda, wearing a neatly creased shirt and tie, Zweig jotted notes as he studied the essays. In these pages, he believed, was the answer to the question that was tormenting him: "Then as today the world torn apart, a battlefield, war raised to the apotheosis of bestiality: in such times the problems of life for man merge into a single problem: How can I remain free?"[40]

The Zweigs had been homeless since 1934. As a Jew, he had had the foresight to flee Austria for Great Britain four years before the German Anschluss. In 1940, however, the Zweigs again packed their belongings when Nazi Germany, having smashed Great Britain's closest ally, France, was preparing to cross the Channel. After a short spell in the United States—where, most improbably of all, he and Lotte lived in a house in Ossining, New York, then home to Sing Sing Prison—they again crossed an ocean to settle in Petrópolis. A wave of German colonists in the second half of the nineteenth century left a linguistic and cultural imprint on the town. But in the Zweigs' bungalow, surrounded by verdant flora and exotic fauna, these echoes from the past made their present more unbearable. "I would not have believed," he reflected in a letter, "that in my sixtieth year I would sit in a little Brazilian village . . . miles and miles away from all that was formerly my life, books, concerts, friends, conversation."[41]

Suddenly, however, Zweig's "discovery" of Montaigne gave him a book, a friend, and conversation. (Concerts would have to wait.) Through his book that, as Montaigne declared, was "consubstantial" with its author, Zweig found a friend. Crucially, this friend's gift for captivating and candid conversation carried Zweig through the final and bleak months of 1941. He devoted these weeks into transcribing his part of the conversation into a small book on Montaigne. In the opening pages, Zweig reveals that the *Essays* were not such a "discovery" after all. He had first read the essays when he was twenty years old but did not know "what to do with them." It was only now, forty years later in a world utterly transformed, that he rediscovered Montaigne: the sixteenth-century Frenchman now appeared as the most vital of interlocutors. "It is for a generation like ours, thrown by destiny into a quickly collapsing world," Zweig wrote, "that the liberty and integrity of his thought brings us precious assistance."[42]

What, then, of Montaigne's behavior during the plague in Bordeaux? Zweig's reply is brutal: "Montaigne fled in panic and abandoned his city." No doubt thinking back to his decision to leave Austria several years earlier, Zweig explained that Montaigne's flight was neither irresponsible nor immoral: "We can no longer comprehend what the plague meant back then. All we do know is what the plague meant to those in its path: flee for your lives." Moreover, again like Zweig, Montaigne had a responsibility to his own family: his elderly mother, his wife, and their one surviving daughter. As his mayoral mandate expired, the best Montaigne could do—for his family's sake and, yes, his own sake—was not expire as well. And so, packing his family, retainers, and manuscript into carriages, Montaigne mounted his horse and fled. These actions, Zweig declares, cost him "a little glory, honor and dignity. But the 'essential' was saved."[43]

On February 23, 1942, with the manuscript just completed and Carnival season just commencing, Stefan and Lotte Zweig retired to their bedroom. They were convinced, it seems, that the Nazi plague would next strike Brazil. And so, they fled one last time. The police found the fully dressed couple together in bed the next day, both of them dead. According to the coroner's report, an overdose of the barbiturate Veronal was the cause of death. As to whether Zweig had also saved the "essential," the coroner did not say. Though Montaigne was not a fan of suicide, perhaps he would have agreed that Zweig also had held fast to the essential. Did he not, after all, do as Zweig declared Montaigne had done? Only those who are "forced to live in an era where madness has overcome the masses, and war, violence and the tyranny of ideologies threaten one's very life and liberty, can understand how much courage, honesty and strength is necessary to remain true to one's true self."

...

After 1585, Montaigne ratcheted up his critique of the native barbarism of his fellow French. And he did so with distinctly un-Pyrrhonian vehemence. "Monstrous war! Other wars act outward; this one acts also against itself, eats and destroys itself by its own venom. It is by nature so malignant and ruinous that it ruins itself with all the rest, and tears and dismembers itself with rage." What, he asks, have we become? In his essay "On Physiognomy," he turns to plague metaphors by way of answer, declaring that "Our medicine carries infection . . . In these epidemics one can distinguish at the beginning the well from the sick; but when they come to last, like ours, the whole body is affected, head and heels alike; no part is free from corruption."[44]

This sense of exasperation with his fellow human beings is not new; we find similar bursts of frustration in the earlier essays. But there is something else that distinguishes the third and last book of the *Essays*, marked by his experience of plague, from the first two books. Whereas the prospect of death hovers over the early essays, the promise of life surges through the late essays. The force of plague, it seems, bent the curve of the essays, away from the preparation for his end and toward a celebration of the life that preceded it. With his life growing short, he seeks to thicken it by dwelling on its everyday pleasures as well as pains. So keen is he on "laying his hands" upon each and every experience left to him, Montaigne has an unlucky servant stay awake at his bedside. His job is to awaken his master as soon as he drifts off to sleep, "so that I might catch a glimpse of it."[45]

In "On Physiognomy," the same essay in which he excoriates both Protestant and Catholic extremists for working toward "our public death," Montaigne now excuses himself from the same schools of ancient philosophy he had formerly attended. If we devote our lives to studying how to die—something that the peasants on his estate do so well without any schooling at all—we would be better off founding a "school of stupidity." The curriculum of such a school is based on everyday experiences and not erudite explications. To enroll in such a class amounts to excluding ourselves from life. By dictating how we should die, these philosophies distract us from living. Death, he allows, is the end of life, "but not the goal of life . . . Life should be an aim unto itself, a purpose unto itself."[46]

In "On Experience," Book 3's concluding essay—or as conclusive as an essay can be for a writer who resists conclusions—Montaigne continues to reflect on diseases. But they are no longer the diseases of religious war or bubonic plague. Instead, he declares that the "most barbarous of our maladies is to despise our being."[47] It is not what will be or what has been that counts, but our being at this moment that we should embrace. With our minds reflexively fleeing ahead or retreating behind our present, this is easier said than done. There is nothing so difficult to learn, the aged Montaigne allows, as "how to live this life well and naturally." The need to unschool ourselves and understand what we thought was natural—trying to climb ever higher, trying to push ahead ever faster—goes against the grain of all our habits. All the more reason, Montaigne believes, that we must habituate ourselves to a different model. It is a model that "regards as great whatever is adequate and shows its elevation by liking moderate things better than eminent ones."[48] Not a model we normally encounter in corporate boardrooms or business schools, but perhaps for that very reason, a model we must essay.

On the last page, Montaigne nestles one of his most celebrated observations: "It is an absolute perfection and virtually divine to know how to enjoy our being rightfully. We seek other conditions because we do not understand the use of our own and go outside ourselves because we do not know what it is like inside. Yet there is no use our mounting on stilts, for on stilts we must still walk on our own legs. And on the loftiest throne in the world we are still sitting on our own rump." But that passage does not end the essay. Instead, after pleading that "old age be treated a little more tenderly," Montaigne concludes with a passage from the ancient Roman poet Horace. In his ode to Apollo, the poet asks that the god grant him health "with mind entire / And not unsolaced by the lyre."[49] It is, I admit, a passage I had always thought to be one too many. How much more effective to finish the essay on one's behind than on a Horatian ode to a Greek god. But now, having reached old age, I admit I was wrong to have thought this. What can be more important than a mind entire and a lyre?

...

"I love you, darling." Each and every time I step into Mrs. R's room, she greets me with this warm welcome. Each and every time, after I reply that I love her too, she then asks, "Do I know you?" Each and every time, I set her tray down on the bed table and smile. "Oh, I think we might have met before." It is my own private Groundhog Day.

It took just two days for me to realize that Mrs. R remembered me for exactly the length of time I spent helping her with her meal. This was a new kind of everyday experience for me. Dementia and Alzheimer's disease were conditions with which I was familiar only through films and documentaries, the stories of friends and accounts in newspapers and novels. My own family's multiple health failings have fallen mostly on those organs lodged in our chests, not the one ensconced in our skulls.

As a result, I tended to joke about dementia in ways I would never dare about emphysema. At least, I did until the day a student came by my office to ask about a recommendation letter that I had promised a few weeks earlier to write for her. Slapping my forehead, I apologized and explained, with a smile, that the good thing about Alzheimer's is that I was always making new friends. The student did not smile back. "Mr. Zaretsky, you told me that same joke last week."

But with Mrs. R, I was free to tell her the same jokes I had told her the day before. I was also free, I thought, to not think too hard about her. She was a large woman whose head was topped by a smattering of white hair and whose facial features, apart from a wart that stood out like an island, were long ago submerged by deep waves of graying flesh. Her inert body was covered by a couple of off-white blankets, sometimes stained by an earlier meal. Though I always prepared her hot meal as quickly as possible, I was never quick enough. While I fumbled with the cellophane covering her plate, the fingers of Mrs. R's left hand—the right one was attached to a paralyzed arm—had already buried themselves in the dish of tapioca pudding that always came with her dinner. Like Montaigne, Mrs. R "made little use of spoon or fork"; unlike Montaigne, she could and did dine very comfortably without a napkin.[50]

While wiping Mrs. R's hand with a napkin, I would glance at the framed photos of her family hanging above her night table or at the talking heads on the flat screen. I would then look at Mrs. R and wonder if there was a *there* there. Was there the "infinite depth and variety" that Montaigne found in himself and, or so I desperately believed, was sloshing around in myself? After a few weeks of mostly unvarying routine, I started to think there wasn't. My dinners with Mrs. R seemed little different from the dinning of voices on the flat screens: the same greetings, the same exchanges, the same good-byes.

One afternoon, as I was cleaning her up and preparing to leave the room, she suddenly asked if I liked music. Surprised, I looked at her and said I very much did. Buried under her blankets and her fingers still sticky with tapioca, with her roommate Mrs. F's oxygen machine thrumming in the background, Mrs. R began to sing in a wavering but lilting voice. "On night guard, I'm a-ridin' round a thousand bedded steers. And tonight my thoughts are slidin' down the trail of distant years." I put down the napkin and looked at her. "Coyotes howling in the darkness soothes my weary bones. The varmints prowling about the campfire make the cowboy feel right at home."

And then, Mrs. R began to yodel. Like Alzheimer's, I had never before in my life encountered yodeling. There was nothing at all operatic, even alpine about these yodels; they were soft and yearning. As they rolled across the room and over the hum of the machine and screen, I turned to look at Mrs. F. Staring at the ceiling, she was smiling. When I turned back to Mrs. R, who had stopped yodeling, I saw that she was also smiling. "Is this my home?" she asked. Stunned, I replied that it was. Her smile widened: "I love you, darling." Walking out of the room with her tray in my hand and her song in my ears, now thinking about the trail of distant years, I replied, "And I love you, darling."

4

DANIEL DEFOE AND THE GREAT PLAGUE OF LONDON

> Man may be properly said to be alone in the midst of the crowds and hurry of men and business. — *ROBINSON CRUSOE*

> The many dismal Objects, which happened everywhere as I went about the Streets, had fill'd my Mind with a great deal of Horror. — *A JOURNAL OF THE PLAGUE YEAR*

Set in front of a white wall and angled toward the floor, a colossal though partly corroded anchor offers one of the more curious sights in Marseilles's municipal museum. Discovered by divers in 1978, it was one of the few salvageable objects from the wreck of the three-mast merchant ship *Le Grand Saint Antoine* outside the city's harbor. Returning from the Turkish port city of Smyrna, the vessel had docked at the port of Marseilles on May 25, 1720, where it unloaded its cargo of precious fabrics.

The ship's subsequent sinking was, however, the work of neither storm nor battle. Instead, it was the work of Louis Philippe, who served as regent following the death of Louis XIV in 1715. Stunned by the news from Marseilles, he ordered that the vessel be set aflame and sunk. The reason was as simple as it was dreadful: stowed away in the folds of exotic textiles carried in *Le Grand Saint Antoine*'s hold was *Yersinia pestis*, the pathogen of the bubonic plague. In a matter of days, residents in the city's poorest quarters began to fall ill and die. Diagnosed by doctors as a "malignant fever," the disease roused the interest of the *échevins*, or municipal officials, when it began to bleed into the bourgeois and aristocratic neighborhoods.

By early July, those with the means began to flee the city. The *échevins* fell over themselves, enacting existing regulations for the sequestration at home of the ill and their families, as well as the collection and burial of bodies at night. Their task became increasingly onerous as the number of dead began to leap exponentially. Incredibly, it was only then that the *Le Grand Saint Antoine* was finally burned, more than two months after Louis Philippe first issued the order. Shortly after, on July 30, the Parlement of Provence made official what most everyone already understood: Marseilles harbored the bubonic plague. The parlementarians issued an order that shut down the city, warning that anyone caught either entering or departing it would be arrested and executed. They outlawed all commerce and communication with the city, closed its gates, assigned guards along the perimeter and, for good measure, locked the city's Jews behind the walls of the city's ghetto.[1]

The local church authorities offered their own prescription to this fearsome visitation. Henri de Belsunce, the city's bishop, was convinced that God was punishing Marseilles for its commercial riches and growing hubris. Belsunce shouldered the full weight of his faith and offered himself as a sacrificial victim to appease God's righteous wrath. Delivering a powerful sermon in the public square near the port, the bishop then walked barefoot across the square with a rope hanging around his neck and his arms cradling a cross. According to a witness, "everyone was struck with a profound pain and they requested the mercy of the Lord."[2]

Yet God seemed less struck. Belsunce survived the plague, but vast swathes of his parishioners did not. The daily toll of deaths during July had hovered around fifty, but the number jumped to more than seven hundred by the end of August. Nevertheless, the plague did not reach its paroxysm until September, when the bodies of more than a thousand men, women, and children were being carted to mass graves every night. At least, that is, when there were carts enough to collect the bodies. As the bishop deplored in a sermon, "We have seen all the streets of this city trimmed on both sides with half-rotten corpses, so filled with diseased rags and furnishings thrown out of windows that we do not know where to place our feet."[3] By 1722, when the pestilential tide had retreated and finally relinquished its hold on Marseilles and parts of Provence, it had claimed almost 120,000 lives out of a population of nearly 400,000.[4] The numbers, already shocking, were made more so because most Europeans believed the plague was a thing of the past. After all, it had not been heard from since 1665 and the Great Plague of London.

...

While the plague did not extend much beyond Provence, news of its improbable but irrefutable existence quickly registered across Europe and the English Channel. Indeed, the British were especially worried by the news. Britain may well have ruled the waves, but the waves—or, rather, the ships that traversed them—ruled the economy. The wealth of the nation was closely tied to the health of its maritime commerce; the decline of the latter, threatened by the plague's reappearance, would invariably entail the decline of the former. Yet could the nation risk such a fatal tariff, an epidemic charged to the goods its ships brought back to their shores? As an Anglican pastor observed in a 1720 sermon, "the channels by which our Riches are conveyed, may convey the Plague to our Houses."[5]

In early eighteenth-century England, to mention the word "Plague," even in a sermon, was incendiary. One might as well shout "Fire" during a performance of Shakespeare at the Drury Lane Theatre. In either case, the natural response was to run for one's life. And for good reason: the contagion of 1665 was cataclysmic. The first signs appeared in June, spurring public unease and the cancellation of an annual event that was famous (or infamous) for its carnivalesque atmosphere: the Bartholomew Fair. Such measures proved inadequate: by September, more than 7,000 Londoners—their bodes ravaged by the bulging of their lymph nodes into buboes—were dying every day. By the end of the year and the retreat of the plague, this city of about 450,000 residents had registered more than 100,000 deaths.

With the memory of the Great Plague still very much alive, a galvanized Parliament, aghast at the pestilential wave surging across Provence, repealed the 1710 Quarantine Act, replacing it with the more robust Quarantine Act of 1721. Too robust, in fact, for a number of parliamentarians. Several members of the House of Lords protested the draconian nature of the new provisions, declaring that while it might suit the submissive French, it would not do for "free-born Englishmen." Several of the measures certainly posed a clear threat to this expansive, if elusive, notion of English freedom. Not only did the Act impose a forty-day quarantine on potentially infected persons, but it also authorized local officials to take any measure necessary to detain these individuals as well as sentence to death anyone who tried to escape their enforced isolation. Moreover, anyone who came into contact with an infected individual was also, "by any kind of violence that the case shall require," to be quarantined. Most dramatically, the king could order the cutting of a deep trench around any quarantined town or village in order to isolate it, as well as the shooting of any individual who, in this "act of felony," attempted to cross it.[6] More than a few "free-born Englishmen" were wondering if George I, the king they had recently imported from Hanover, had mistaken who his subjects now were.

...

Following the parliamentary and public debates with sharp interest was a sixty-year-old Londoner who had, during his long life, spent time in prison for seditious writings and also served various governments as a spy; founded successful businesses yet also made disastrous investments; championed the cause of religious dissent while alienating scores of dissenters. Pilloried three times in his long life, he was also pardoned by two different monarchs. Few contemporaries lived so momentous a life, one that hurtled from triumph to terror, and left a lasting mark on him. On more than one occasion, he might well have moaned "In the Middle of all this Felicity, one Blow from unforeseen Providence unhing'd me at once."

In fact, he did say this, albeit through his fictional creation Robinson Crusoe. Rather improbably, as average life expectancy in eighteenth-century England was less than fifty years, Daniel Defoe had also just published his first novel, the wildly successful *The Life and Adventures of Robinson Crusoe*. By the time he reached an age when many of us prepare for retirement from the world, Daniel Defoe was instead preparing to engage it with renewed force. What he has Crusoe say of his life serves as the epitaph of his own life and adventures: "I must have made very little use of my solitary and wandering years if, after such a scene of wonders, as my life may be justly called, I had nothing to say, and had made no observations."[7]

Born in London in 1660, Defoe was a child during the Great Plague. Yet, we do not know if he remained in London during that awful event. For a man who wrote millions of words—by one count, nearly three million between 1722 and 1731—Defoe was strangely tight-lipped about himself.[8] With few surviving documents or letters, we know little about his early years; even his date and place of birth are circumstantial. It is possible, though, that Defoe was packed off to the countryside when the plague crashed on the city he would later describe as that "great and monstrous thing."[9]

If Defoe did have memories of this visitation, sights he perhaps glimpsed as a child, they resurfaced with the news from France. Raised as a Nonconformist—Protestant dissenters who, rejecting the rites of the Church of England, were burdened by an array of civil disabilities—Defoe naturally interpreted these new clauses to the Quarantine Act as autocratic. Then as now, the question of individual rights versus collective obligations arose. How great a reach should a government, especially one inspired by democratic principles, have over the lives of its citizens? In the popular *Applebee's Original Weekly Journal*, Defoe offered an answer of sorts. Behind one of his many literary pseudonyms, he underscored the appalling consequences of extreme laws by dwelling on the nature of the French government's fierce quarantine of Toulon, a port near Marseilles. Besieged by the plague, the city was ringed by royal soldiers ordered to prevent residents from fleeing. When several hundred men and women, driven by hunger, nevertheless tried to escape, the soldiers opened fire, killing nearly two hundred and wounding more than a hundred others. "Among the first were three and thirty Women and Children, and four and fifty among the latter," Defoe reported, "so that most of them were driven back into the City, where they must inevitably perish."[10]

The sad irony to the taking of innocent lives in order to save yet other innocent lives is that it did nothing of the sort. Defoe noted that several hundred civilians nevertheless "got over the Lines and spread themselves everyway over the Fields." While most would have been tracked down and shot by the soldiers, even a few escapees, if stricken by the disease, sufficed to undermine the blockade's purpose. As Defoe's contemporaries read his account, their thoughts must have skittered between horror at what took place in France and horror at what might take place at home. All the more so, as the account strives for accuracy, especially when the writer underscores that full accuracy remains beyond his reach. He thus notes that the desperate rebels "attempted the Lines in sixteen *or* [my emphasis] seventeen Places." He is also careful to qualify certain statistics, prefacing his statement that 137 women and children were wounded with the phrase "as they say." Defoe does not make clear who "they" are or where he found these numbers. What he does make clear, though, is that when it comes to statistics, we can't live with them and we can't live without them.

...

During mealtimes at the home, the residents and I often gaped at the so-called dashboards—the displays of data tracking the progress of the disease and tally of the deceased, the number of swabs jammed up noses and the count of patients plugged into ventilators—that appear, like a game show visual, during the daily briefings by local officials. I tried to avoid commenting on the statistics, telling myself that they were just that, statistics, meaning little to the residents. Was it not better this way? Did they really need to know that I heard on the car radio on my way to work one day in early April that our state ranked second to last in testing and tracing? For every 100,000 Texans, slightly more than 300 were being tested—just about the number of students sitting in an auditorium for my lectures in the pre-pandemic era.[11] Was it really possible to reach more Texans with a lecture on Homer's *Odyssey* than with a nasal swab or phone call?

When it came to meaningful numbers at the residence, they

mostly fell into single digits. Number of cookies served with dinner. Number of pills given by the nurse. Number of days passed without a bowel movement. Number of nights passed lying in dirtied gowns and shirts. More rarely, the numbers rose into double and even triple digits—for example, the number of pieces to a puzzle. While the scarcity of toilet paper and disinfectant worried the administrators, the scarcity of puzzles worried several residents who passed the days piecing together pictures of flowers blooming in vases, puppies scampering on floors, and Adam reaching toward God. Within days of the lockdown, there was an online run on puzzles, their prices rising as crazily on eBay as tulips did in seventeenth-century Holland.

But puzzle-mania made more sense than did tulip-mania. The residents could not bake bread or plant gardens, after all, so they turned to puzzles to fill those hours they once spent in group activities. From time to time, a family miraculously procured a puzzle, sending it to their relative at the home. But as with yeast and flour, so too with puzzles: the supply could not catch up with the sudden and unexpected demand. The residents were reduced to circulating the puzzles; they would find themselves putting together and taking apart the same puzzle they had worked on the week before. Frankly, I was not even sure if they recalled that the pieces they emptied from a box were the same pieces they had emptied into the box a short while before.

Yet the dashboard numbers did not pass unremarked by the residents. They saw them as tokens of what was unfolding outside the residence, of events that cut them off from their families, cut them off from one another and, for those hoping to return to their homes, cut them off from hope as well. (In a way, the numbers also explained—if that is the word—why I was sitting by their bed, trying to convince them to eat a spoonful of overcooked green peas. For the residents, I appeared more or less at the same time as did the odometer of death on the small screens.) But it was not, I think, numbers alone that impressed them. Instead, it was how the numbers were couched by city officials and talking heads. The word "exponential," for example, seemed to carry an extraordinary punch. Whenever this word was mentioned by a health official, I noticed the residents would often open their eyes wider than usual.

Many of the staff were concerned not just by the specter of exponential growth in numbers, but also by the reliability of those numbers. Some state Republicans claimed that health officials were overcounting COVID-related deaths, while many epidemiologists worried that those same officials were instead undercounting the number of fatalities. The chaos was, in part, systemic. Our death certification system, like so much else in the Lone Star State, is decentralized. Just a few of the more than 250 counties have medical examiners, which means that justices of the peace are called in to determine the cause of death. This leaves a lot of room for ideology or ignorance to slip into their calculations. Even those justices who strove for accuracy were often hobbled for more prosaic reasons. Several counties, I learned, were not testing the dead for the coronavirus because their offices were too financially strapped to do so. For those who have never been to Texas, it is hard to explain this system. But take it from one of my favorite residents, Mrs. T, who worked as a safety officer at oil drilling sites: it ain't worth spit.

...

For Defoe, death certification in London wasn't worth spit, either: *A Journal of the Plague Year* repeatedly questions the Bills of Mortality. Beginning in the late sixteenth century, the Company of Parish Clerks provided weekly tallies of the number and causes of death in each of the nearly 100 parishes that constituted London. Most often, the "searchers" who categorized and counted the dead were not physicians or apothecaries, but older women, usually working in tandem and paid for their pains by parish officials. Though not formally trained, these searchers often brought experience as nurses or midwives to their job. They could also rely on popular manuals like *A Watch-Man for the Pest*, published in 1625, which instructed its readers that one sign of a plague victim is "great trouble and oppression of the Heart, that the Partie unquietly rowles up and downe for rest from one Place to another."[12]

One virtue of statistics, at least in seventeenth-century England, was that their precision calmed the "trouble and oppression of the Heart" created by otherwise unpredictable events. They provided certainty in an uncertain world, an epistemological anchor that kept individuals from being swept away in the whitewater of experience. The apparent incontrovertibility of statistics consoled; by quantifying the future, they contained fears; by drawing on patterns from the past, they proposed plans for the future. A few years before the outbreak of the Great Plague, a member of the Royal Society, John Graunt, undertook a statistical analysis of the Bills of Mortality, making use of recent advances in mathematical probability made across the Channel by Blaise Pascal and Pierre de Fermat. As if overnight, statisticians were offering a wild range of projections, from the profitability of life annuities to the probability of divine providence.[13]

Yet Defoe was a dissenter not just with regard to the Church of England, but also with regard to the church of statistical science. He did not dismiss the utility of the mathematical models, but he doubted the reliability of the raw evidence used by statisticians. Over the course of 1721, as he pored over the Bills of Mortality, his doubts deepened. By February 1722, with the publication of his manual *Due Preparations for the Plague, as well for Soul as Body*, Defoe became convinced that nothing was less certain than the Bills of Mortality's credibility. "By the Judgment of all that have been seriously in that Matter, the Bills of Mortality neither did, nor was it possible as Circumstances were known then to be, that they shou'd give a full Account of the Numbers of People that perish'd in that dreadful Calamity."[14] Rather than the official figure of 68,590 deaths, Defoe was convinced the actual number was as high as 100,000.

He was alarmed, in particular, by the propensity to cite statistics to bolster what we wish to believe and not what we need to know. In one of the manual's many dialogues, a man tells his younger brother that people, desperate to avoid being shut in their houses, were bribing the searchers to lie about the cause of death of their family member. Yet the young brother refuses to believe him. "How can you suggest such a thing, Brother? There is no room for it, the Number is known as every Body is allowed to see it." Then, for good measure, he adds, "I take things always for true when Authority publishes them."[15] One need not be a Dissenter, like Defoe, to be disturbed by this common refrain. And it is in order to reveal the reasons for his dissent that Defoe turns not just to numbers, but also to narratives.

...

In early September 1664, Londoners first heard that the plague had arrived in Holland. The stories, seeded by letters written by merchants and sailors, quickly sprouted across the city. The anxiety following in the wake of these rumors was met by yet other rumors that the government had plans afoot to prevent the disease from reaching Britain. By the end of November, however, the rumors of pestilence became reality when the city learned that two men had died of plague in the neighborhood of Drury Lane. Though their family sought to hide these deaths, two physicians sent by local authorities to investigate found "evident Tokens of the Sickness upon both of the Bodies that were dead [and] gave their Opinions publickly, that they died of the Plague."[16]

So begins the journal of H.F., the fictional saddler harnessed by Defoe to tell the tale of the Great Plague. As any businessman worth his salt, H.F. knows his math. Scarcely a few pages into his account, he makes the first of dozens of references to the Bills of Mortality. He does so, in part, to track the movement of the plague. Mirroring the disease's ebb and flow during the winter months of 1664–1665 is the ebb and flow of hope and fear among the residents. By May, however, as the numbers start to climb at a quickening pace, fear finally overtook hope. Indeed, there was no need to read the Bills of Mortality to see what now seemed a hopeless situation. As searchers combed the houses, they found that "the Plague was really spread every way, and that many died of it every Day: So that now all our Extenuations abated, and it was no more to be concealed, nay it quickly appeared that the Infection had spread itself beyond all hope of Abatement."[17]

Like a dirge's basso continuo, the bills weave through H.F.'s narrative as spring stretches into summer and the plague strengthens its grip on London. What the numbers fail to reflect, though, are the lives of those swept away by events. By mid-June, panic becomes a constant presence, spurring those with the means to pack up their households and flee the city. For those who lack the means or money to leave, a sense of fatalism sets in. As corteges of carriages and carts that "throng out of Town" lengthen, H.F.'s melancholy deepens. The sight, he writes, "filled me with very serious Thoughts of the Misery that was coming upon the City, and the unhappy Condition of those that would be left in it."[18] The events that H.R. will witness over the next several months concern less the city of London than they do the poorer quarters of London. As a witness, his task is not just to count the deaths of the poor, but to show why those deaths counted.

By August, as the mortality figures surge in the poorer districts, the city itself shifts in character. "The Face of London," H.F. notes, "was now indeed strangely alter'd." Emptied of life, the city's face seemed drained of blood. It was the same city, but one "all in Tears." Though the plague had yet to reach all parishes, they had nevertheless mostly been abandoned. The results were unnerving, an anticipation of our own era's postapocalyptic films where the buildings still stand but their residents have disappeared. The streets, H.F. marvels, "usually so thronged, are now grown desolate and so few People to be seen in them, that if I had been a Stranger, and at a Loss for my Way, I might have gone the Length of a whole Street . . . and see no Body to direct me."[19]

More distressingly, those "few People to be seen" most often were the Watchmen—the men tasked with the miserable job of guarding infected homes. They were not posted to guard against those who sought to break in, but instead against those who sought to break out—the families who now found themselves trapped inside. This was, undoubtedly, the most alarming element to the new quarantine policy imposed by city officials in late June. It announced a long list of prophylactic measures, ranging from the banning of "Bear-baitings and singing of Ballads" to the prohibiting of "publick Feasting." But the law that figured most prominently was the shutting up of infected houses. The detail that horrified Londoners was that not only was the infected individual closed inside for a month, but so too were all those who came into contact with that unfortunate person. For good measure, the shuttered houses were marked with a large red cross on the door, captioned by the words "Lord Have Mercy Upon Us."[20] These were less a warning for others to keep away than an epitaph for those locked inside.

...

Though not trained as a scientist, Defoe always took care to follow the science. He has H.F. do the same, as when he acknowledges that the principle of quarantine is sound. While the etiology of the bubonic plague was a mystery—it was only during the 1894 outbreak in Hong Kong that scientists discovered that the plague bacillus was carried by fleas riding on black rats—there was less mystery over the connection between contagion and commerce. The forty-day quarantining of ships suspected of carrying the disease had been practiced in Europe as early as the mid-fourteenth century, when the Black Death began its first sweep across the continent.[21] In fact, the very word "quarantine" came from *quaranta*—the forty-day isolation period imposed by Venetian officials on all ships docking in their harbor.

Then as now, however, differences arose over the meaning of "following the science." The quarantine policy, particularly the practice of shutting up entire families, outraged not just those married to the myth of the freeborn Englishman, but also those appalled by the policy's sheer cruelty. For critics like Defoe, it was more than a moral crime, it was also a policy blunder. He has H.F. observe that despite the "Cheques" put in place, the number of dead continued to spiral unchecked. As a result, H.R. roundly condemns the refusal of authorities to discriminate between the "Sound" and the "Sick." The policy "looked hard and cruel; and many People perished in this miserable Confinements, which 'tis reasonable to believe, would not have been distemper'd if they had had Liberty, tho' the Plague was in the House."[22]

In the end, H.F. roundly condemns the policy as not just inhumane, but also utterly ineffectual. "It is doubtful to this day, whether in the whole it contributed anything to the stop of the Infection, and indeed, I cannot say it did; for nothing could run with greater Fury and Rage than the Infection did when it was in its chief Violence, tho' the Houses infected were shut up as exactly and as effectually as it was possible."[23] H.F. cannot overemphasize the futility and cruelty of this policy; it was beyond the power of the officials "to prevent the spreading of the Infection . . . the shutting up of Houses was perfectly insufficient for that End. Indeed, it seemed to have no manner of publick Good in it, equal or proportional to the grievous Burthen that it was to particular Families that were so shut up."[24]

Not only was this particular policy perfectly insufficient, H.F. contends, but so too were the statistics used to justify them. He presents a damning list of charges against the data gathered by the searchers. It is less that they were liable to bribes to mislead the authorities than that they were limited as to what they could accomplish. At the height of the plague, the searchers and parish clerks could no more render accurate counts of the dead than they could give accurate counts of snowflakes during a blizzard. It was already difficult to concentrate on the counting of the dead when your own name might be added to the list by day's end. It was yet more difficult to count when the inhumane conditions created by the plague made any human activity nigh impossible.

...

Before leaving for my first day of work, I carefully wedged the residence's official appointment letter between the dashboard and windshield. As I drove along nearly empty streets, I kept glancing from the rearview mirror to the letter for reassurance. Stupidly, I half expected to be pulled over by the police, demanding to know where I was going. On March 19, Governor Abbott had signed the executive order that mandated the closure of dine-in restaurants, schools, and nursing homes. On March 24, local officials had upped the ante by issuing a stay-at-home order. By then, my university had beaten a retreat—a stampede, really—from classrooms to computers. Rather suddenly, I found myself more or less shut in the house with my family.

Once I arrived at the residence and signed dozens of legal documents, the director of nursing introduced me to T., a certified nursing assistant, or CNA. She had been given the task of teaching how to help the "feeders"—the name given to those residents who, for a variety of physical and cognitive reasons, could not feed themselves. In order to ease me into my job, T. chose Mrs. L as my test case. Not only did Mrs. L seem perfectly lucid, but she was perfectly grand. When we walked into her room, Mrs. L was sitting upright in her bed. In her late eighties, she wore a long mane of white hair that, carefully swept back, cascaded along her sharply chiseled face. Mrs. L's azure eyes and bright pink lips, arched in a smile, were set off by porcelain skin. It was as if Thomas Gainsborough had arranged her features.

As T. set down the food tray, crowned by a plate of chicken strips, mashed potatoes, and green peas, on the bedside table, she confided in a stage whisper that Mrs. L had once worked for Columbia Records in New York City. Her smile widening, Mrs. L nodded her head. "Oh, yes, I did," she told me, adding, "And I met Frank Sinatra." Bent over her, nervously tying her bib as T. looked on, I straightened up and blurted: "Sinatra? Seriously?" She nodded again: "Yes, Frank Sinatra." "How wonderful!" I again shouted while T. reminded me to remove the cellophane from the glass of iced tea and cup of tapioca pudding, then cut the chicken into manageable pieces. Looking serenely out the window, Mrs. L. replied, "He *was* wonderful." By then, I had seated myself next to her. Struggling to spear a few green peas with the fork, I sent them instead pinballing across the tray, a few ricocheting off Mrs. L's bib. "Looks like I'm doing it my way," I muttered. T. laughed while Mrs. L looked at me. "Yes, he was wonderful," she whispered, smiling.

Over the following weeks and months, Mrs. L never lost her smile. Even with the mask she wore while wheeling herself along 300 Hall, the smile was revealed by the deepened wrinkles around her eyes. Slowly, however, it seemed to empty of its original import and fill with a new meaning. One afternoon in late May, when the home had been in lockdown for more than two months, I was trotting down 300 Hall on my way to the kitchen for desperately needed packets of Splendora. Passing Mrs. L's room, I saw her lying in bed, the food tray untouched and her mask slightly askew. I braked by her door and asked how she was. She looked at me but did not seem to recognize me. Adjusting my mask and walking toward the bed, I looked at her closely. For the first time, I saw a few clusters of gray hair jutting from her chin. "So, tell me again about Frank," I asked Mrs. L while I straightened her mask. Looking at me, she nodded her head, but didn't reply. I think she smiled. But there was something confused, not wonderful, behind the smile. Upon saying good night and heading to the kitchen, I could not help but wonder if Mrs. L was losing her way.

...

H.F. tried to align his way with God's way. As the residents of the wealthier parishes ran from the city, his thoughts mostly ran in circles. Should he go or should he stay, was the confounding question he repeatedly asked himself. Wrestling with himself, H.F. reflected that he "began to consider seriously with my Self, concerning my own Case, and how I should dispose of my Self." Inevitably, his considerations were as much spiritual as they were practical. Though a bachelor, H.F. knows that a "Family of Servants" depends upon him. Could he leave them—or for that matter the shop and warehouse filled with his goods—behind and unprotected? Yet, at the same time, his brother, who has already sent his own family from the city, keeps reminding him that the one and only certain protection against the plague is to run as soon and fast as possible.

While irresolute, H.F. is also impressed by his brother's urgency. He tries to find a horse to ride from the city—by then a fool's errand, as there are no more horses in London than there are Londoners prescient enough to have already purchased them. At the same time, the servant he had planned to take with him, frantic over H.F.'s waffling, leaves on his own. Other obstacles, or what are perceived as obstacles, appear in H.F.'s way, preventing him from quitting London. Are they obstacles, H.F. wonders, or oracles—tokens of a different sort, heralding not death but divine guidance? Is, in fact, London calling?

His brother, more skeptical and less patient, will have none of this. The only signs H.F. must consider, his brother insists, are the mounting numbers of dead recorded by the Bills of Mortality. As a result, H.F. comes home one night "greatly oppress'd in my Mind, irresolute, and not knowing what to do." In a fascinating illustration of probability theory in the guise of Christian casuistry, H.F. urges his readers to do what he is attempting to: undertake a "Conscience of his Duty." Namely, the task of keeping "his Eye upon the particular Providences . . . and look upon them complexly, as they regard one another, and as altogether regard the Question before him, and I then think he may safely take them for Intimations from Heaven of what is his unquestion'd Duty to do in such a case."[25]

Casuistry is no longer what it was once cracked up to be. When used today, it suggests a kind of ethical sleight of hand—seeking excuses for the inexcusable. Yet, while it already had this taint in the early eighteenth century, casuistry still held its original sense: the application of the general rules of religion and ethics to particular and particularly knotty cases. Defoe often drops his characters, from Robinson Crusoe to Moll Flanders, into such seemingly irresolvable situations, forcing them—and, of course, us—to use such reasoning to find their way to a resolution. This activity reflects, as G.A. Starr argues, Defoe's deep conviction in our moral agency. We are free, but also duty-bound beings for whom moral deliberation constitutes "the very stuff of daily existence. Experience is a constant challenge, since action involves choice and choice involves responsibility."[26]

Rather than abandoning this practice in extreme situations, it becomes all the more essential. Time and again, H.F. faces situations that force him to weigh, as a man of reason and faith, the available choices. Yet his faith dominates, especially in the scene, steeped in Augustinian imagery, when H.F. makes his final decision. With surprise, he realizes that while his mind had been occupied by sorting through the various arguments, his hand had been flipping through his copy of the Bible. He decides to choose a page at random; whatever page and passage he alights on will be the answer to his irresolution. Opening the book, his eyes fall on Psalm 91, in particular the passage that warns of pestilences to come and comforts those who find shelter in God. From that moment, H.F. resolves to stay in London, convinced that God was "as able to keep me in a Time of the Infection as in a Time of Health."

And yet, the following morning he wakes up ill. So ill, in fact, as to be bedridden and besieged by fears that his casuistical calculations have condemned him. After three days, however, H.F. begins to recover from his illness and his fears soon subside. Whatever the cause of his malady, it was not the plague. Yet this is not, by a long stretch, the last time the foundations of his shelter of faith will be shaken by frightening events. So very frightening at times, he confides, that the weight of regret over not having left London grows impossibly heavy.

...

By mid-July, H.F. confesses that the "many dismal Objects, which happened everywhere as I went about the Streets, had fill'd my Mind with a great deal of Horror, for fear of the Distemper itself, which was indeed, very horrible." As he walks the city streets, H.F. witnesses the torment of the infected Londoners who, unlike him, were too poor to leave the city. Driven mad by the pressure of the buboes in their groins or necks, men and women threw themselves from their windows or into the Thames. Others, squeezed in the disease's vise, "vented their Pain by incessant Roarings, and such loud and lamentable Cries that would pierce the very Heart."[27] It is that same heart, H.F. confesses, that now felt faint and failing as he "sorely repented of my Rashness in abiding to remain in Town."

Yet, if one seeks horror, there is no better stage than the "great and monstrous Thing." Like the protagonist of a Gothic horror story, H.F. wanders a London cloaked in a thick film of the uncanny and unspeakable. When he sees others, he fears to approach them, worried they belong to what he calls "THE WELL." Playing on the word's two meanings—a shaft reaching a deep underground supply of water and an adjective denoting those who are in good health—THE WELL is those who had "received the Contagion, and had it really upon them, and in their Blood, yet did not shew the Consequences of it in their Countenances." THE WELL is, in short, THE ASYMPTOMATICK: "dangerous People whom the well People ought to have been afraid; but then on the other side it was impossible to know them."[28]

The dread of the unknown and unseen seeps into all of H.F.'s daily activities. Drawn despite himself to scenes best avoided and to peer into places best ignored, H.F. returns to his house so terrified that he vows never again to step outside. The problem is that he repeats this vow time and again during the course of the plague. Because he cannot "prevail upon my unsatsify'd Curiosity to stay within," his resolution repeatedly evaporates, and he again ventures outside. His curiosity is never disappointed: tumbling across the pages are terrifying tableaux in which people die in a "Variety of Postures" too dismal to describe. Yet more terrifying are those tableaux where he cannot see the victims but can clearly hear them. In one scene, H.F. recounts that as he crossed by the aptly named Token-House-Yard, "a Casement violently opened just over my Head, and a Woman gave three frightful Skreeches, and then cry'd *Oh! Death, Death, Death!* in a most inimitable Tone, and which struck me with Horror and a Chilness, in my very Blood. There was no Body to be seen in the whole Street, neither did any other Window open; for People had no Curiosity now in any Case; nor could any Body help one another; so I went to pass into Bell-Alley."[29]

Yet the most dreadful scene unfolds at a burial pit. Like the thuds of the lifeless bodies dumped into these awful craters, H.F.'s images resound. You *hear* the words as Defoe makes darkness not only visible, but also audible. Passing the pit in the parish of Cripplegate one night, H.F. cannot overcome his curiosity and is drawn slowly to its edge. Upon reaching it, he is struck nearly dumb: I cannot, he writes, give "a true Idea of it to those who did not see it, other than this: that it was indeed very, very, very dreadful, and such as no Tongue can express." H.F. sees several Buriers gather around a man, clearly agitated, who had also appeared at the pit's lip. Though they urge him to leave while he can still stand, the man explains he has come only to witness the burial of his entire family, who were just tossed like cords of wood onto the Dead Cart. Leaving the man to watch, the Buriers proceeded to turn around their wagon, whereupon "the bodies shot into the Pit promiscuously." Overwhelmed by the sight, the man cries and collapses to the ground. The Buriers, no less overcome despite having become inured to such sights, escort the grieving man to a nearby tavern.

Yet, the horror does not end there. Once the man is led away, H.F. notices that the Cart carries more bodies. "Some were wrapt up in Linen Sheets, some in Rugs, some little other than naked, or so loose, that what Covering they had, fell from them, in the shooting out of the Cart, and they fell quite naked among the rest; but the Matter was not much to them, or the Indecency much to anyone else, seeing they were all dead, and were to be huddled together into the common Grave of Mankind, as we may call it, for here was no Difference made, but Poor and Rich went together."[30]

Every death, Inga Clendinnen reminds us, "is its own discrete catastrophe. Within the mass of the only apparently anonymous we must seek and hold the individual action, the individual situation."[31] While Clendinnen's focus is on depictions of the Holocaust, her insight applies to other instances of mass death. Defoe's narrator cannot fully express this scene, for no human being can. But H.F. comes very close by depicting a mass of barely distinguishable corpses viewed by a living person desperate to make those very distinctions. As we listen to that man's sobs, we become that father, that husband, straining to see the remains of his wife, his children. The catastrophe, because it is discrete, becomes recognizable: it becomes fully human. We then understand that it is not just curiosity, but the duty of bearing witness that pulls H.F. toward these unbearable scenes.

In effect, H.F. never loses sight of his duty, which is to remain fast not just to his God, but to his fellow men and women. They are mostly the city's poor who, condemned to stay in London, are consigned by need to take the most dangerous jobs. They cannot take refuge in their homes, as they cannot afford to remain without work. The same lack of means that stops them from fleeing also steers them into becoming essential workers like the Bearers, who collected the dead, and the Buriers, who dispatched them. They sought this work, H.F. observes, out of sheer need and suffered, from repeated exposure, the inevitable consequences. "Innumerable of the Bearers dy'd of Distemper, infected by the Bodies they were oblig'd to come so near; and had it not been, that the Number of poor People who wanted Employment, and wanted Bread, was so great, that Necessity drove them to undertake any Thing, and venture anything."[32]

Yet H.F. recognizes these individuals, even as their labor and losses threaten to make them unrecognizable. The portraits veer, at times, toward the grotesque. Gazing at one man who lost his family, H.F. writes that this father and husband was "so absolutely overcome with the Pressure upon his Spirits, that by Degrees, his Head sunk into his Body, so between his Shoulders, that the Crown of his Head was very little seen above the Bones of his Shoulders; and by Degrees, losing both Voice and Sense, his Face looking forward, lay against his Collar-Bone, and cou'd not be kept up any otherwise, unless held up by the Hands of other People."[33]

At other times, his portraits verge on the sublime. One day,

H.F. walks toward the Thames, curious to see if there were fellow Londoners who had reacted to the plague by retreating to ships docked off the banks. What he finds, instead, is a man who, working as a waterman, is firmly docked to his humanity. Identifying himself as Robert, the man tells H.F. that his wife and children are infected, yet still alive in their house. When a shocked H.F. demands to know how he could abandon his family, Robert replies: "Oh sir, the Lord forbid! I do not abandon them; I work for them as much as I am able and keep them from Want." Every night, Robert explains through his tears, he makes what money he can from delivering goods to the ships, then leaves what food he can afford near the house for his wife. At that very moment, H.F. sees Robert's wife appear at the door of the house and, with one of their little boys, steal out to gather the goods. At a safe distance from one another, Robert and his wife exchange words of thanks to God, upon which she and the boy return to the house with their meager meal. While H.F. cries in recollecting the scene, we recollect the reasons for the cries and collapse of the man at the burial pit.[34]

...

Along with moments of compassion and concern, however, H.F. also evokes scenes of callousness and corruption. Indeed, instances of selflessness often seem dwarfed by scenes of self-preservation. For every Robert the Boatman there are many others, like those who pretend to be physicians, intent on profiting from the misery of their fellow Londoners. H.F. marvels at the multiplying number of notices promoting phony and often dangerous cures. "It is incredible, and scarce to be imagin'd, how the Posts of Houses, and Corners of Streets were plaster'd over with Doctors Bills, and Papers of ignorant Fellows; quacking and tampering in Physick, and inviting the People to come to them for Remedies."[35] When they were not hawking "INFALLIBLE preventive Pills" and "INCOMPARABLE drinks" against the plague, these charlatans were instead touting magical charms and amulets. When H.F. discovers that people were purchasing pitch and tar, or rosin and brimstone as cures, he exclaims that he "cannot but take notice that the strange Temper of the People of London at that Time contributed extremely to their own Destruction."[36] Torn between despair and disgust, he is left to wonder how "the poor People found the Insufficiency of those things, and how many were afterwards carried away in the Dead-Carts."[37]

Yet these "Quacks and Mountebanks," many of them carried off by the very disease they promised to cure, reflected a deeper crisis. Defoe may have read Thucydides; his description of the implosion of social practices in London neatly parallels the Greek historian's account of the Athenian plague.[38] But it may well be that while there are many ways to report such mass mortality events, all these ways issue from the same harsh reality. Both writers reveal how the plague's gale-like intensity scarifies the landscape of human activity, leveling into rubbish the social practices and religious rituals whose sturdiness we had taken for granted. In both Athens and London, temples empty of the faithful while streets fill with their corpses. H.F. tells us that some ministers "did visit the Sick at first . . . but it was not to be done; it would have been present Death, to have gone into some Houses: the very buryers of the Dead, who were the hardest Creatures in Town, were sometimes beaten back, and so terrify'd that they durst not go into Houses, where whole Families were swept away together."[39]

The plague stripped society to its bones, baring a world of naked self-interest and preservation, a world where man is seen to be what he truly is: a wolf to other men. Defoe shared with

Hobbes the same starting point in his account of human nature. We are driven, both believed, to dominate others. As Defoe declares in his epic poem *Jure Divino*, it is thanks to this "Tincture in the Blood" that "All Men *would be Tyrants* if they cou'd."[40]

At times, however, even words like "tyrant" fail to capture the harrowing actions—most often heard of and not seen—that H.F. reports. It is not just that man becomes a wolf to man; it is that families become wolves to one another. "But alas! This was a Time when every one's private Safety lay so near them, that they had no Room to pity the Distresses of others; for everyone had Death, as it were, at his Door, and many even in their Families, and knew not what to do, or whither to fly. This, I say, took away all Compassion; self-Preservation indeed appear'd here to be the first Law. For Children ran away from their Parents, as they languished in the utmost Distress: And in some Places, tho' not so frequent as the other, Parents did the like to their Children."[41]

Most despairingly, even the experience of the plague fails to purge this "tincture" from the blood of Londoners. When the plague crashed over the city in the spring of 1665, its impact initially forced people to forget their religious and political differences. Yet when the pestilential tide subsided with the arrival of winter, H.F. sighed that "Things returned to their old Channel again."[42] Not only did those who had fled the city rush back to reopen their shops and restart their social activities too soon—actions that, as the Bills of Mortality reflect, led to a sharp rebound in deaths—but there also sprang back "the Spirit of Strife and Contention, Slander and Reproach, which was really the great Troubler of the Nation's peace before."[43] The memories of what H.F. calls the "Terror of those Times" decayed more quickly, it seems, than the tens of thousands of bodies thrown into the pits. King Charles II and his court, who H.F. affirms had failed to plan for the plague and did little to protect their subjects once it arrived, returned from their Oxford exile to London and their life of garish spectacles and lavish spending. With dreams of power, political factions were again maneuvering against one another, while religious factions were again circling one another with loathing. As for the people of London, they "soon cast off all Apprehensions" and, indeed, all thoughts about what they had survived.

H.F. refuses to bring his account to a conclusion, instead offering a "coarse but sincere Stanza":

A dreadful Plague in London was,
In the Year Sixty Five,
Which swept an Hundred Thousand Souls
Away; yet I alive!

Having put right the numbers and put forth his narrative, H.F. invites all of us who are now alive to draw our own conclusion.

5

ALBERT CAMUS AND *LA PESTE BRUNE*

> The confrontation between the administration, which is an abstract entity, and the plague, which is the most concrete of all forces, can only lead to comic and appalling results.
>
> He who has hope for the human lot is a fool, but he who despairs of events is a coward.
>
> ALBERT CAMUS

In 1939, Albert Camus was a young man all revved up but still unsure where to go. A native of French Algeria's capital city, Algiers, Camus had recently graduated from the local university. His thesis, on the writings of Saint Augustine and the neo-Platonist thinker Plotinus, was less remarkable than the fact that Camus had the occasion to write it. Raised by an illiterate, semi-deaf, and largely mute mother who worked as a cleaning woman, Camus was not the sort who reached high school, let alone university. Yet thanks to teachers, in particular Louis Germain, who took notice of the boy's intellectual promise, Camus had taken a university diploma—and promptly found himself unemployed.

Living in a communal house with several other idealistic twenty-somethings, Camus dithered over a career in teaching before ditching the provincial position he was offered. He then threw himself into political engagement, joining the Communist Party in 1935, only to be thrown out a short time later due to his refusal to toe the ideological line. After a stint of odd jobs, Camus next joined a newly launched local newspaper, *L'Alger Républicain*, where he filed investigative pieces blasting the local administration's mistreatment of Arab and Berber communities. His reward was a local reputation as a rebel who, thanks to his articles, again found himself jobless when the French authorities shut down the paper.

But this was only the most visible side to Camus's life as a writer. By 1939, he was drafting not one, but three different books: the novel *The Stranger*, the philosophical essay *The Myth of Sisyphus*, and the play *Caligula*. Branding it the "cycle of the Absurd," Camus used all three genres as vehicles for his pursuit of meaning. As he declared with the audacity of hopelessness in the opening of *The Myth of Sisyphus*, there is "but one truly serious philosophical problem, and that is suicide. Judging whether life is or is not worth living amounts to answering the fundamental question of philosophy."[1] The urgency of the question becomes nearly unbearable when the various answers essayed by Camus always lead to the absurd. Though this word has since calcified into a cliché, its original meaning cannot be ignored. For Camus, the absurd happens when the world meets our desire for true and lasting meaning with definitive and deafening silence. Absurdity is not the desert we traverse in our search for meaning, but the dry crackling we hear during our passage. "The absurd depends as much on us as on the world. For the moment that is all that links them together."[2]

The consequence of our absurd condition is exile. When we persist in justifying our world even with false reasons—those provided by theology or ideology, for example, or those encouraged by thoughtlessness or laziness—we remain in a familiar world. But sooner or later, Camus writes, the stage set collapses. The world we were given and the illusions that furnished it evaporate, making us strangers in a newly strange world. We become, in effect, displaced, condemned to an "exile that is without remedy since we are deprived of the memory of a lost home or the hope of a promised land."[3] Where are we to find meaning? If we cannot discover a transcendental guarantee for a purposeful life, what are we to do? Is it possible, Camus wonders, "to live without appeal"?[4]

When France declared war on Germany in 1939, this question took on sharpened significance. With the government's shutting down of *L'Alger Républicain* because of its muckraking and the shutting off of military enlistment because of his tubercular lung, Camus traveled to Paris in early 1940 to take a job on another newspaper, the evening tabloid *Paris-Soir*. He despised the paper's sappiness, despaired over the city's grayness, and was driven mad by the government's senseless claims that France would win the war against Germany because it was stronger.

But when the six-month-long *drôle de guerre*, or phony war, suddenly lurched into a very real war with the eruption of German panzer divisions into France in May, Camus and the rest of France confronted a shattering instance of the absurd. Several million men, women, and children, civilians as well as a growing number of soldiers, surged onto the roads in motorcars, horse-drawn carts, bicycle, and foot, uncertain of where they were going, yet desperate to keep ahead of the Germans. This time, it was not an individual stage set, but a national stage set that had collapsed. How many men and women, as they struggled southward and gazed at an empty sky, under which strafing Stukas might suddenly appear, asked themselves, "Why?" Camus perhaps knew better than to ask. Driving a company car, he made it as far as Lyons, where he remained after France signed a humiliating armistice with Nazi Germany. He witnessed, with shock and disgust, the establishment of an authoritarian, antisemitic, and collaborationist state in the spa town of Vichy under the elderly World War One hero Marshal Philippe Pétain. By year's end, a struggling *Paris-Soir* reduced its staff and a suddenly redundant Camus was forced to return to Algeria without any job prospects, but with a bright and beautiful wife, Francine Faure, he had begun to court shortly before the outbreak of the war.

...

Absurdity can burst into being regardless of time and place, but certain places and times seemed especially propitious for its appearance. Take the city of Oran, as Camus suggests. French Algeria's second biggest city, Oran is a little more than two hundred miles west of Algiers. Like the capital, Oran is a port city, but that, at least for Camus, was where the similarities ended. He made this ruthlessly clear with a long essay titled "The Minotaur, Or Stopping in Oran," which he completed in 1939. A visitor, he announces, will find streets "reserved for dust, pebbles and heat," empty cafés with "grease-covered countertops strewn with the feet and wings of flies," and storefronts offering an "edifying abundance of undertakers." The principal pastimes of the city's young men are "having their shoes shined and promenading in these same shoes" along the dusty and hot boulevards. Comparing the city to a labyrinth, its streets lined with ugly buildings and its back turned to the sea, Camus asks: "Emptiness, boredom, an indifferent sky: what enticements do these places offer? Solitude, doubt, and perhaps human beings."[5]

It was in pursuit of Francine that Camus had made several visits to Oran in 1939, and it was to Oran that the newly married couple returned in early 1941. Camus's hatred for the city was now compounded by his dependence on the kindness of the Faure family. Without two sous to rub together, he had no choice but to agree to move into an apartment owned by Mme. Faure and adjacent to her own apartment. When Camus was not revising the manuscripts for his cycle of the absurd, he gave private lessons to Jewish children barred from attending public schools. He lambasted Vichy's vileness and lamented his exile from Algiers. In a letter to a former professor and friend, the writer Jean Grenier, Camus bemoaned that he found himself trapped in the suffocating maze he had mocked in his earlier essay. "You would not believe the isolation one can find in Oran. It's a savage and burning labyrinth . . . It's so extreme it can be exciting. But sometimes we need civilization. And this desert has no oasis."[6]

Yet if this desert did not offer an oasis, it did offer Camus the inspiration for his next cycle of works. By the spring of 1941, at the very moment a typhus epidemic was sweeping through the nearby region of Tlemcen, short references to plague began to appear in Camus's journal; by the early fall, they had grown into long passages, many drawn from his readings of earlier accounts of plague. In an early draft, Professor Philippe Stephan, a character who does not survive the subsequent revisions, praises Thucydides as a man who had "experienced the affliction" that he also described in clinical detail.[7] Camus also took notes on a recent French translation of Defoe's *A Journal of the Plague Year*. Tellingly, though, *Robinson Crusoe* had also marked the young French Algerian, who plucked a line from the novel as the epigraph to his own slowly forming novel: "'Tis as reasonable to represent one kind of Imprisonment by another, as it is to represent any kind of Thing that really exists, by that which exists not."

Camus's life in Oran came to feel even more like an imprisonment when, one night in May 1942, he was suddenly racked by spasmodic coughing, his mucus darkened by blood. A doctor hurriedly called to the apartment informed Camus that his tuberculosis had spread to his second lung. His choice was stark: either remain in Oran, whose climate would worsen his condition, or temporarily move to a drier and cooler climate. Camus knew he could not stay in Oran and, thanks to Faure family connections, found a suitable situation in Le Panelier. It was little more than a knot of farmhouses near Le Chambon-sur-Lignon, a village located in the southeastern corner of the harsh and arid Massif Central. While the village, situated some three thousand feet above sea level, was predominately Protestant, it also was home to Catholics and Darbyists, a Protestant denomination that, unlike traditional Protestantism, did not believe that God's covenant with Christians superseded his covenant with Jews. It was a world apart from the sun-blasted and sea-bordered world of Oran, not to mention Algiers.

Given the agonizingly slow process of applying for the necessary travel documents, it was only in early August that Camus, still weak and accompanied by Francine, crossed the Mediterranean and reached the isolated hamlet. Upon settling at the farmhouse, Camus continued to take notes for the novel, but also of his new setting. The rising morning sun over the small and craggy mountains, he observed, made it seem that their covering of fir trees cascaded toward the valley: "the outbreak of a brief and tragic battle in which the barbarians of daylight will drive out the fragile army of nocturnal thoughts."[8] Among these nocturnal thoughts, no doubt, was not just his physical condition, but also the moral condition of France. "Plague," he wrote in the preceding journal entry: "Impossible to get away from it." Was he thinking of the occupation of his lungs by a dangerous bacterial strain? Or the occupation of France by an equally dangerous ideological strain? As with the sun igniting the glow of fir trees, these entwined experiences lit his thoughts. *The Stranger*, he noted, had depicted "the nakedness of man facing the absurd." But, he continued, his new novel would "show that the absurd *teaches nothing*. This is definitive progress."

The inability of the absurd to teach us anything became even clearer in November. By then, Francine had returned to Oran and her teaching position and winter had come to Le Panelier. In early November, however, there was another arrival: the Germans. In response to Operation Torch, the Allied invasion of North Africa, the Germans extended their military occupation to the so-called Free Zone, roughly the southern half that included Camus's isolated hamlet. In an entry dated "*11 novembre*," Camus scrawled: "*Comme des rats!*" To be sure, he was now trapped like a rat in France. But this was not the only meaning carried by this image.

…

A half-dozen pages into *The Plague*, Camus introduces us to the story's protagonist—and, we eventually discover, narrator—whose place is in Oran. At the same time, though, he introduces us to something out of place in Oran. "Upon leaving his clinic on the morning of April 16, Dr. Bernard Rieux felt something soft under his foot. It was a dead rat lying in the middle of the landing. On the spur of the moment he kicked it to one side and, without giving it a further thought, continued on his way downstairs. Only when he was stepping out into the street did it occur to him that a dead rat had no business to be on his landing."[9]

From this first encounter, the horror mounts. Soon, it is not one, not hundreds, but thousands of dying rats bursting from the city's bowels, lurching across the streets and sidewalks, and collapsing next to the bloated and bleeding bodies of their dead brethren. The sight was sickening, of course, but also unsettling, as if they were heralds of an unthinkable yet unstoppable fate crowding upon the city. Picture the consternation of our town, Rieux observes, "hitherto so tranquil, and now, out of the blue, shaken to its core, like a quite healthy man who all of a sudden feels his temperature shoot up and the blood seething like a wildfire in his veins."[10]

The association between the black rat and bubonic plague is as old as the plague itself. When he was still in Oran, Camus received what he jokingly called his "pestiferous books"—a package of scientific works that a friend, Lucette Maeurer, had sent him from Algiers.[11] Among these works was one by Proust—not *that* Proust, but instead Marcel's father Adrien Proust, a well-known epidemiologist who in 1897 published *La défense de l'Europe contre la peste*. In his wide-ranging survey of plague epidemics, Proust noted an "interesting fact": pestilences were often announced by invasions of dying rats. In Canton, for example, neighborhoods counted as many as 20,000 dead rats, the advance sign of what was in store for the unhappy residents.[12]

Recent studies suggest that the black rat has been wrongly accused of complicity with the Black Death. Instead of disease-bearing fleas hitching rides with rats, the guilty parties might well have been fleas or lice carried by human beings.[13] Archaeologists have not found the number of rat skeletons from the fourteenth century that would signal their pivotal role in the disease's transmission, while epidemiologists suspect that so-called "rat falls"—the waves of dying rats associated with plague—are limited to the modern era. For now, all of this is conjecture; what remains a fact, though, is that, along with fleas clinging to its fur, the rat also carries all sorts of signifiers. They are never happy meanings. Long before a causal relationship between rats and disease was established, Hans Zinsser notes, "mankind dreaded and pursued these animals."[14]

This is, of course, even truer for the plague itself. In his notebooks, Camus declared that the plague "has both a social and metaphysical sense."[15] The former sense refers to *la peste brune*, or "brown plague," the phrase used to describe the German occupation. But the metaphor of plague cannot be limited to a particular color or connotation. Of course, as Camus made explicit several years later, the plague signified the Nazi presence not just in France, but in all of Europe as well. But while it was no less than that, he continued, it was also much more than that.[16] Already in 1942, Camus grasped that the affliction that had struck the French in 1940 had existential ramifications. "What I wish to express through the plague," Camus wrote in his notebooks, "is the sense of suffocation from which we all suffered, and the atmosphere of menace and exile that we all experienced. At the same time, though, I wish to extend this interpretation to the general notion of existence."[17]

...

"Help me! Help me!" When I first heard this piercing scream from 300 Hall, I was loping to the kitchen in order to fetch packets of sugar for a resident. I froze in place and looked up and down the hall. With the regularity of a police siren, the same words, as sharp as glass shards, kept ricocheting down the hall. It was my second day at the residence, and I half expected to see a scene from *ER*, with a gurney manned by doctors and nurses careening past me to the rescue. Instead, I saw a nurse chatting with an aide, while another aide, entering information about one of the residents, was methodically tapping on a nearby wall screen. Puzzled by their lack of response to the persistent cries,

I turned to the aide at the screen, whispering that these calls sounded important. “No, it sounds like Mrs. N,” she replied, without breaking her rhythm at the screen.

Looking up and down the hall, I saw that no one else seemed prepared to do anything more than roll their eyes. I walked toward Mrs. N’s room and peeked across the threshold. Seated in a reclining chair at the far end of the room, a small woman drowning in a baggy flower-print gown, deep red veins lacing her face and a plastic oxygen tube dangling from her nose, fixed a set of wild eyes on me. Her thin arms, protruding like bare twigs from a stunted bush, stretched toward me from the gown’s folds. “Help me, help me!” Stepping closer, I asked what was wrong. Her lungs? Her heart? Her bladder? “It’s on the floor!” she shrieked. Staring under her chair and table, I was becoming as frantic as Mrs. N. “What’s on the floor?” I cried out. “This!” As she jabbed with a half-fisted hand toward her feet, I realized that Mrs. N suffered from rheumatoid arthritis. Catching sight of the object of her jabbing—a crumpled napkin—I realized that Mrs. N’s mind, like her hands, was no less knotted, though by dementia.

When I picked up the napkin and placed it on her table, it was as if I had flipped a switch. Suddenly, Mrs. N’s desperate cries for help ended, replaced by frantic shouts of “Thank you, thank you!” Gesturing toward the spot where I picked up the napkin, she cried, “It was on the floor!” It *was* on the floor, I agreed. Gently, I added that that wasn’t a reason to scream for help. Though she sharply nodded her head, it was not clear that she agreed, or even understood what I had just said. As I walked quickly out the door and past the aides and nurse, Mrs. N continued to shout her thanks. While embarrassing, her gratitude also buoyed me. I felt virtuous and, yes, superior to the rest of the staff. Unlike them, I insisted on paying attention to Mrs. N not despite, but *because* of her piercing screams over what was so inconsequential to me, but of the greatest significance to her. Basking in the high esteem I held for myself, I loped even faster to the kitchen for the nearly forgotten sugar packets.

The next day, the esteem began to whistle out of me like helium from a balloon. I had just delivered the evening meal to Mr. B in Room 302. Though blind, Mr. B enjoyed listening to episodes of *The Andy Griffith Show*, which I had discovered seemed to cycle endlessly on one of the cable channels. While my eyes darted from the screen to the fish sticks I was cutting into small pieces, the sudden wail of "Help me, help me!" stopped me in mid-slice. Mr. B sighed and, with the remote gripped in his hand, raised the volume several notches. I got up, telling him that I had to step out for a moment and help another resident.

I walked rather than trotted to Mrs. N's room. She was sitting in the same position in the same chair, her face contorted in the same expression of uncontrollable panic. Upon seeing me, she pleaded more loudly for help. When I asked what was wrong, she violently gestured to her rolling table. "What's wrong with the table, Mrs. N?" Jabbing toward the table, she cried, "This!" As there was only a water mug and landline phone on the tabletop, I asked if she needed more water. "No! This!" That left the phone. "It isn't working?" I asked. "It's in the wrong place!" she cried. Following her hand gestures, I pushed the phone sightly to her right. Once again, the panic subsided as quickly as it started, followed by an explosive "Thank you!"

By the end of the first week, I realized that Mrs. N's frantic calls for help were as common as the loudspeaker calls for this nurse or that therapist. To my shame, I also realized that I began to pay as much attention to the screams as I did to the garish Impressionist knockoffs on the hallway walls. When busy in other rooms ladling a spoonful of green peas onto a waiting tongue or passing out packets of sugar as if they were contraband, Mrs. N's screams, like the paintings, became part of the decor. Sometimes, to my shame, I rolled my eyes in mock exasperation when I passed a nurse or aide. There she goes again, as predictable and propulsive as Old Faithful. Only after I was through with my tasks did I trudge to Mrs. N's room in order to pick up or shift whatever was out of place. I would also remind her that there was no need to scream over a used Kleenex or straw wrapper. Looking into her vein-streaked eyes livid with panic, I knew such reminders were pointless: she could not understand me. Or, if she could, she could not act upon this understanding.

But I continued to remind, even reprimand her. It is only now, as the year draws to a bleak end, that I grasp that I did so because I refused to understand her. How could I ever do that? The prospect of attending to Mrs. N's dread and distress, anxieties and afflictions, was a bridge too far for me. Was I not being good enough by being in the nursing home in the first place? Besides, it was so much easier to believe that Mrs. N, though enfeebled and near her endgame, could conform to my world. No need, then, to make the effort to enter her world. I learned last week that this particular world has now gone silent: a friend at the residence told me that Mrs. N died of COVID-related complications. Despite the residence's best efforts, Mrs. N could not be helped in the end.

...

Camus often did things by five in his writings. In *The Stranger*, the protagonist Meursault shoots "the Arab" five times. In his play *The Just Assassins*, there are five acts. In his philosophical essay *The Rebel*, there are five sections. It happens that in classical French tragedy—for example, the plays of Corneille and

Racine—there are five acts. For Camus, tragedy—and all of these works are, to one degree or another, tragic—is divisible by five.

Inevitably, the most tragic of his works, *The Plague*, also has five parts. In the first part, the scene—Oran—and time—1940s—are established, the rats are unleashed, and the principal characters are introduced: Bernard Rieux, Jean Tarrou, Joseph Grand, Raymond Rambert, Father Paneloux, and Cottard. As the doctor in the time of plague, Rieux naturally occupies the tragedy's center. Rieux is all the more central because he is the teller of the story. But is it *une histoire*—which means both story and history in French—or something else altogether that he tells? At times, Rieux describes himself as a historian; at other times, though, he describes his account not as a history, but instead as a *chronique*, or chronicle. The choice of words reflects a choice of narrative values. While a *histoire* implies the presence of an author who creates and shapes the story, a *chronique* suggests the absence of such authorial control. In the latter, unlike the former, events impose themselves without the chronicler establishing causal or even moral connections.

Rieux makes this distinction not just at the start of his account, but also in the middle and at the end, each time repeating his criteria for telling a story *pas comme les autres*. He reminds us that he describes only those events he has either witnessed, heard about from others, or read in relevant documents he has found; he reminds us that he has aimed at objectivity and impartiality; he reminds us that he avoids making changes for artistic effect. In this *histoire qui n'est pas une histoire*, he also reminds us that he "refrained from attributing to his fellow sufferers thoughts that, when all is said and done, they were not bound to have."[18] In effect, Camus has Rieux remind us that he has read Thucydides, who presented the same criteria to the readers of *his* history—including his famously confounding claim that he has his historical figures say what they *should* have said. As was the case with the ancient Greek tragedian, so too with his modern French Algerian counterpart: by laying claim to objectivity, both are inviting us to step into their stories by making our own causal and moral connections.

Indeed, for Rieux, there is a vital connection between morality and language. To express oneself clearly and truthfully is, quite simply, a moral duty. When Rambert, a Paris journalist, tries to interview Rieux about the living conditions of the local Arab and Berber communities, the doctor, who knows the conditions are wretched, asks if he could publish "an unqualified condemnation of the present state of affairs." When Rambert demurs, Rieux refuses the interview. He has no truck, he explains, "with injustice and compromises with the truth."[19] So, too, with the plague. Rieux has resolved to fix "his mind on observed facts" (39), to "lucidly recognize what had to be recognized" (40) and "do his job as it should be done" (41)—even or especially when that job, whether in diagnosing a bacterial or ideological pestilence, demands real facts and relentless clarity. "What is the ideal for a man prey to plague?" Camus asks in his journal, warning his imaginary interlocutor that they "will laugh at the answer." It is, quite simply, "honesty."[20]

This same ethical imperative holds for Rieux's comrades. An obscure government clerk who devotes his free time to trying to write, Grand has striven for years, without success, to find the words to "render perfectly the picture in my mind's eye [so that] from the very first words it will be possible to say, 'Hats off!'" (104–105). Tarrou is forever scarred by his youthful experience of witnessing his father, who was a prosecutor, condemn a man to death. His father, Tarrou recalls, "spewed out long, turgid phrases" that hid the act's enormity or substituted abstractions like "the supreme penalty" for the reality of separating a man's head from his body. Ever since this experience, Tarrou has come to understand that "all our troubles spring from our failure to use plain, clear-cut language" (254). In one of his sermons, even Paneloux, a Jesuit who prides himself on his erudition, refuses "an eloquence that, considering the tragic nature of the occasion, would be out of keeping" (99). Of the five, only Cottard, refused a first name by the narrator, refuses to tell the truth about his dubious past. Ominously, he remarks that he wishes he were a writer—though not to educate others, he adds, but instead to control them.

Tellingly, Cottard alone rejoices over rather than resists the plague. Indeed, he collaborates with this pestilential occupation. As the actions of Rieux, Tarrou, and the others make clear, there is a common thread to seeing, speaking, and acting rightly—a thread that binds them so tightly as to make them nearly indistinguishable. Once the city is quarantined, these individuals gravitate toward Rieux, thickening into a kind of resistance. A stranger to Oran, Tarrou pays a visit to Rieux in order to propose the creation of voluntary sanitation squads. This, in turn, allows Rieux, who immediately agrees, to propose the ethical imperative that determines his response: "I've never managed to get used to seeing people die" (128). When Tarrou points out that the doctor's successes will, at best, always be temporary, Rieux finishes his visitor's thought: his efforts mean "never-ending defeat."

Yet this stops neither Rieux nor the others who join him in his struggle. When the journalist Rambert finds himself trapped in Oran, he pleads with Rieux to provide him with a pass to leave the city and return to Paris, where he had left his fiancée. When Rieux demurs, Rambert explodes: "But I don't belong here." True enough, but irrelevant. As Rieux replies matter-of-factly, "Unfortunately, from now on you'll belong here" (86). Refusing to accept this diagnosis, Rambert pursues every possible (and, of course, illegal) means to escape the city. Several weeks later—a period marked by a wildly spiraling mortality rate—the chance for Rambert to slip out of the city finally appears. Yet he turns it down, instead casting his lot with those resisting the plague. His reason is telling: "Now that I've seen what I have seen, I know that I belong here whether I want to or not" (209).

For those resisting the plague, morality is thus a matter of seeing clearly. Tarrou echoes this value when he recounts his courtroom experience to Rieux. While his father spoke in abstractions, Tarrou looked at the criminal whose head, thanks to his father's eloquence, would soon fall: "He looked like a yellow owl scared blind by too much light. His tie was slightly awry, he kept biting his nails, those of one hand only, his right . . . I needn't go on, need I? You've understood—he was a living human being" (247). Dwelling on a detail—the man was biting the nails of one hand—Tarrou then specifies that it was the *right* hand. The detail makes clear that, unlike his father—or, indeed, most of the rest of us—Tarrou saw *that* man with the bitten nails of the right hand, the same nails that would continue to grow, at least for a short while, after his head was removed. (A decade earlier, George Orwell made the same use of detail to convey the enormity of taking a life. In his vignette "A Hanging," he describes his experience as a colonial officer in Burma, assigned to assist at a hanging. He watches a "puny wisp of a man with a shaven head and vague liquid eyes" shackled and marched to the gallows by six imposing guards. At a certain point, the condemned man, who was about to die at the end of a noose, suddenly sidestepped a puddle on the path. Till that moment, Orwell writes, he had not "realized what it means to destroy a healthy, conscious man."[21])

Tarrou, Rieux, and Rambert all find the words—written or spoken—to convey the moral imperative of seeing the world as it is. For their comrade in arms Joseph Grand, however, matters are less straightforward. This downtrodden clerk struggles to find his words—a peculiarity, Rieux insists, that is "really the key" to his personality (45). Grand could not find the words, by writing to his superior, to improve his miserable professional lot, nor could he find the words to explain himself, by letter, to the dissatisfied wife who had left him years earlier. No less remarkably, he could not find the words to complete the opening paragraph to the novel he had been working on for years. As Grand blurted to a bemused Rieux, "Oh, Doctor, how I'd like to learn to express myself!" (46).

And yet, when invited by Rieux to join the sanitation team, Grand says yes "without a moment's hesitation" (134). The absence of hesitation seems to me crucial. Though Grand lacks the words to convey what he has seen, the clarity of his vision leads to the clarity of his action. It is as if the two actions—seeing and acting—occur simultaneously. Acting does not so much follow seeing as it instead accompanies it. This is the particular moral quality of sight underscored by the philosopher and novelist Iris Murdoch. "It is a *task*," she writes, "to come to see the world as it is." The reason it is so hard to see rightly, she explains, is because our "fat relentless ego" always blocks our sight. "The difficulty is to keep the attention fixed upon the real situation and to prevent it from returning surreptitiously to the self with consolations of self-pity, resentment, fantasy or despair."[22]

This is the same task at which all of the novel's characters struggle. The temptations of self-pity and resentment blind Rambert at first as he seeks to escape Oran, just as the longing for fantasy blind the city's administrators when they initially refuse to call the plague by its name. Indeed, even Rieux hesitates, if only for a moment, to name the plague until prodded to do so by a fellow doctor. Yet this is not the case with Grand, whose behavior Rieux tries to diagnose. He does not want, he tells the reader, to exaggerate the actions of such volunteers by citing their "courage" or "heroism." Doing what they had to do, they are to be congratulated no more, Rieux argues, than "a teacher on teaching that two and two make four" (132). Of course, there will always be times, now as then, that doing what one has to do—on affirming that two and two equals four—can be dangerous, even deadly. Yet this does alter, Rieux concludes, "knowing whether two and two do make four." Upon acknowledging—*seeing*—this objective truth, every else follows. Or, more accurately, unfolds at the same time. The old chestnut "Seeing is doing" is suddenly invested with new meaning.

...

In his address at a Holocaust remembrance ceremony in 2009, President Barack Obama evoked the six million Jews murdered in the death camps, but also the five thousand Jews saved in an isolated French village. "Not a single Jew who came there was turned away or turned in. But it was not until decades later that the villagers spoke of what they had done, and even then, only reluctantly."[23] The town, Le Chambon-sur-Lignon—the same town down the road from Le Panelier—had by then achieved iconic status on both sides of the Atlantic. It was the village where—as the philosopher Philip Hallie announced in the title of his influential book—goodness happened.[24]

Goodness did indeed happen in Le Chambon. The actions undertaken by these men and women were truly extraordinary, yet they were also threaded with a number of fairly ordinary motivations. Hallie's account, which has deeply shaped popular (and presidential) perceptions of Le Chambon, focuses almost exclusively on the role played by the pastor André Trocmé and his Protestant flock in rescuing Jewish refugees. Over the past twenty years, though, historians have complicated the picture. They have explored the divisions between leaders and flocks on the proper response to the refugees, located Le Chambon's activities in a much wider web of complicity and collaboration, and discovered that Catholic and even local Vichy officials and police also participated in these clandestine operations.[25]

They have also revealed the ties between ethical and commercial hospitality. The farmhouse where Camus stayed at Le Panelier was part of the growing local tourism business. While the region's principal economic activity had long been the cultivation of the soil—a hardscrabble occupation in the best of times—it had, more recently, turned to the more profitable cultivation of vacationers. The seasonal rise and fall of Le Chambon's population reflected the impact of this new industry: while the number of residents dipped below one thousand during the winter, it ballooned beyond six thousand during the summer, attracting families from nearby cities eager for fresh air and clear vistas.

As a result, the line between the tradition of hospitality and the trade of hospitality grew blurred and, at times, volatile. During the Spanish Civil War, the widening river of refugees spilling north over the Pyrenees was not always embraced with open arms. Some refugees who reached Le Chambon at times found that their reception depended on the season. When rooms were at a premium during the summer months, the locals were more reluctant to welcome the refugees.[26] A few years later, the ambivalence of some locals to the thickening stream of Jewish refugees, both foreign and French, prompted town leaders to express their concern: "One can hope that the local businesses and all the strength of the Protestant anthill will be devoted to the sacred cause of the children. Tourism might suffer as a result, but Le Chambon will have fulfilled the mission that

God clearly gave the town."[27] In a way, Le Chambon became the site of safety for Jews for the same reason Vichy became the site of government for the French state: both towns had professional interests in hospitality and lots of rooms to rent.

The initial responses, in sum, were all too unexceptional, all too human. By and large, it was not until the summer of 1942 and the great *rafles*—coordinated sweeps and deportation of foreign and French Jews by French police at the order of the French state—that the people of Le Chambon fully grasped the enormity of events. What was exceptional, though, was the town's response to these events. From this point, the entire population either participated in or kept silent about the clandestine efforts to hide Jewish refugees and, when possible, led them to safety. The individual reasons for these actions were often complex, and the risks taken were death-defying. Saints were in rare supply, but this was not only to be expected, but also to be accepted. As Magda Trocmé, the wife of André Trocmé, observed, "Good and evil are always mixed up. Nowhere is it ever all the way white or all the way black. Here it was something like an acceptable grey."[28]

Most telling, to my mind, is that when researchers asked local residents why they saved Jewish lives, the response was often a stubborn or confused silence. When a respondent did offer an explanation, it was rarely elaborate or elegant. For example, the documentary filmmaker Pierre Sauvage asked one resident, Emma Héritier, why she took in and hid Jewish refugees. After a long pause, she replied with some discomfort, "I don't know. Because we were used to it."[29] As one of the local pastors, Marc Donadille, remarked: "We were people who had work to do, and that work grabbed you by the guts. And what we attempted to do, mostly, was to forget what we knew."[30] For reasons of internal security, silence attended the saving of these lives; for reasons of moral clarity, silence followed the accomplishment of these efforts. As Murdoch affirms, there is "nothing odd or mystical . . . about the fact that our ability to act well 'when the time comes' depends partly, perhaps largely, upon the quality of our habitual objects of attention."[31]

...

What Camus knew about these activities and what he himself did during his stay at Le Panelier is complicated. As his principal biographers, Herbert Lottman and Olivier Todd, make clear—though the former more explicitly than the latter—Camus took no part in any Resistance activity while living in Le Panelier. His time was mostly devoted to reading literary and scientific works on plague, writing early drafts of the novel, and taking the train to the nearby city of St. Etienne to receive pneumothorax treatments for his plagued lungs. The impression left by the industrial city—"Such a sight is the condemnation of the civilization that produced it"—was as painfully deflating as the device that collapsed his lung in the hope of repairing it.[32]

Apart from his dreary visits to St. Etienne, Camus rarely ventured beyond the limits of Le Panelier. Yet there were occasional visitors, including the biblical scholar André Chouraqui, an old friend from Algiers who, stripped of his teaching position because he was Jewish, was living in semi-clandestine circumstances in a nearby village. During their occasional conversations over couscous, Chouraqui revealed to Camus the various meanings of plague in different biblical passages, but kept veiled—here, again, silence imposed itself—his underground activity helping refugees cross the Pyrenees into Spain and on to Portugal.[33]

Two other visitors to Le Panelier were Pierre and Marianne Lévy, who had taken Fayol as their name to hide their identity.

Like Chouraqui, Pierre Lévy was also an active *resistant* who does not seem to have told Camus about his underground activities. He listened to Camus damn Vichy for the deportation of Jews, while Marianne listened to Camus speak about the pain he felt in his separation from not just Francine, but his entire world.[34] Not surprisingly, his notebook entries during this time revolve around the twinned themes of separation and exile. In a note for the novel, Camus writes: "The separated people perceive that in reality they have never ceased, in the first phase, hoping for something: that letters would arrive, that the plague would end, that the absent one would slip into the city. It's only in the second phase that they no longer hope."[35]

Yet separation is imposed not just by microbes, but also by men. Perhaps through conversations with Chouraqui or the Fayols, or through the static of BBC broadcasts, Camus learned the details of the Paris *rafles*, when the French police carried off thousands of Jewish men, women, and children to temporary deportation camps. One was established in an unfinished apartment complex in the suburb of Drancy, the other in the Vélodrome d'hiver, an indoor bicycle-racing stadium in the city proper; both were bereft of medical and material supplies, and both became sites of indescribable horror.

The accounts that reached Camus bled into his initial sketches of the "isolation camps." "The relatives are already separated from the dead—then for sanitary reasons children are separated from their parents and the men from the women. So that *separation becomes general.* All are forced into solitude."[36] In his description of an isolation camp, Rieux relies on an account he finds in Tarrou's journal, one that dwells less on the physical than on the psychological suffering. As he inspects the camp, Tarrou discerns "suspicion in the eyes of all. Obviously, they were thinking there must be some good reason for the isolation inflicted on them, and they had the air of people who are puzzling over their problem and are afraid" (240). As for Rieux, though he lacks firsthand knowledge of the camps, this does not free him of responsibility toward those interned in them. Like so many others, he ventures close enough to the high walls and armed sentries to experience the "smell of crowded humanity, the baying of the loudspeakers in the dusk, the air of mystery that clung to them, and the dread they inspired" (243).

The brutal reality of the occupation—the feeling of exile and fact of separation, the ferocity of officials and fate of a people—in turn inspired Camus to plumb more deeply the notion of the "absurd." He had no illusions over what such a task entailed. It is so hard to go over and, if necessary, go beyond certain beliefs you once held to be right and true. "Let's suppose a philosopher," Camus wondered, "who after having published several works declares in a new book: 'Up to now, I was going in the wrong direction. I am going to begin all over. I think now I was wrong.' No one would take him seriously anymore. And yet he would then be giving proof that he is worthy of thought."[37]

In the novel, several characters marshal the intellect and will necessary to begin all over again. Rambert decides his place is in Oran, and Tarrou grasps that he carries the pestilence. In addition, Paneloux, after witnessing the tormented death of a young boy who was given an experimental serum, comes to a radically different understanding of faith. Grand is the odd man out. This government clerk seems so insignificant that Camus does not even mention his name in his notes for the novel. But insignificance, as Camus observes in a later essay by that name, is not the same as meaningless.[38] In fact, Grand is the most significant character in the novel: unlike the others, he always knew what had to be done. All he needed was the opportunity—the invitation, really—to act upon it. When Rieux asks if he will join the sanitation team, Grand agrees without a moment's thought about the risks. Embarrassed by the doctor's gratitude, Grand replies, "Why, that's not difficult! Plague is here and we've got to make a stand, that's obvious. Ah, I only wish everything were as simple!" (134).

An admirer of Camus's writings, Murdoch cites his novels as examples of how literature, unlike philosophy, helps us "rediscover a sense of the density of our lives" and "arms us against consolation and fantasy." To do this, she adds, prose must recover its former eloquence. It is an eloquence she connects with the effort "to speak the truth," one that makes her think "of the work of Albert Camus."[39] I wonder if Murdoch, while reading *The Plague*, connected Grand to her ravishing insight into the activities of seeing and doing. "If we consider what the work of attention is like, how continuously it goes on, and how imperceptibly it builds up structures of value around us," she writes, "we shall not be surprised that at crucial moments of choice most of the business of choosing is already over."[40] As Grand would have added, "Hats off!"

...

Were he alive today, Grand would no doubt add, "And masks on!" When I first arrived at the residence, I confess I did not wear a mask while doing my rounds. In fact, the bunny head was the one and only time during those first weeks that, if only inadvertently, I avoided breathing on the residents. I was not alone. In the confusion of messages from public health officials over the efficacy of masks, most of the staff did what I did by not wearing them at all. Perhaps a kind of magical thinking was at play—that by refusing masks we could pretend the virus did not exist, or at least was not interested in us. Or, perhaps, we were just lazy and dumb.

Yet more than inertia or ignorance was at work. I noticed that one of the physical therapists—an impossibly attentive and active woman known by one resident as "Blessed Abundance"—came to work one day with a mask. The following day, however, the mask was gone. When I passed her in a hallway and asked what had happened to her mask, she shot me a sad and serious look. The director of nursing, she whispered, had told her the mask was frightening her patients. She sighed and walked quickly off to the gym.

To be honest, the director had a point. It took much less than wearing a bunny head to cast fear among the residents. Attached to their routines and accustomed to the same faces at the same times and same days, they were sensitive to the slightest change; if the Andy Griffith show was not on at the usual hour or the chicken soup was not served on the usual day, their world shuddered slightly on its axis. More than a shudder, I suspect, rippled through the residents when masked women and men first began to step into this same world.

Moreover, one of the most important things the staff—especially someone as otherwise useless as me—brought to these men and women was words. Words of cheer and sympathy, of course. Words about the weather (still hot!) and words about the evening meals (still cold!). Words that, moments after I spoke them, were forgotten by a resident. Or words that, Dada-like, were freed of my original meaning. (When I was serving dinner one night to Mrs. E, a beautiful ninety-year-old who was serene and senile, I recalled hearing she once owned a dude ranch in the Hill Country. As I dipped into ketchup a fork holding a piece of chicken filet, I asked Mrs. E if she had a favorite horse. Looking at me with translucent blue eyes, she replied, "I'm already married.") Words I often shouted at residents with blunted hearing, blasting televisions, or both. The prospect of doing all of this while masked left all of us wordless.

But all of this changed in a matter of days. In mid-April, the wearing of masks was mandated at nursing homes and our magical thinking gave way to manic scrambling. Here as elsewhere, the demand swamped supply and masks became scarcer than bottles of Belgian beer at a Texas icehouse. Weeks earlier, my wife, Julie, with her preternatural prescience, had bought several packages of surgical masks (as well as enough red beans, spelt flour, and cans of coffee to keep us fed and caffeinated until 2030). But other staff members, in particular the aides and housekeepers, lacked the resources to be as resourceful as Julie. They wore what they could, often bandanas, while most nurses and administrators managed to secure surgical masks. One nurse dazzled the rest of us when she appeared with a KN95 mask—already a rare item—that, seemingly customized, had more valves and intakes than a Pontiac GTO.

Though initially unsettled by the sight of masks, the residents soon adjusted. I did as well, mostly by shouting and gesticulating like a madman standing by a traffic light at a downtown intersection. Far more difficult, though, was the adjustment asked of the residents when, a few weeks later, they too had to wear masks. Already deprived of their communal meals in the dining room and soon to be deprived of the gym for their therapy (and gab fests), most of the residents were flustered by the masks. Naturally, they did not wear them during their meals. No less naturally, they did not wear them, or wear them properly, before or after meals. The masks would hang from a single ear, dangle below their chins or, confused with napkins or tissues, sit crumpled on their bedside tables. At times, when I tried to fit the mask over their mouth as gently as possible, all the while trying to explain why this was important, they seemed resigned, but not always understanding.

In fact, I was not always understanding, either. I wondered if, in trying to guarantee their lives, I was instead guaranteeing their isolation and separation from the world that remained to them. It was, I think, the sort of tragic situation introduced by the ancient Greek playwrights and embraced by Camus. In 1943, he wrote in his notebook: "What makes a tragedy is that each of the opposing forces is equally legitimate, equally entitled to exist."[41] The residence lacked the epic scale of Camus's Oran, not to mention Sophocles's Thebes, but it too knew its share of tragedy.

...

Like Grand, Camus never doubted what was right and wrong during the occupation, but he needed an invitation to act upon this knowledge. In his case, the invitation was presented by Pascal Pia, the crusading editor who had a few years earlier hired Camus as a reporter for *L'Alger Républicain*. Shortly after the German occupation of the Free Zone, Pia joined the Resistance movement Combat and met a few times with Camus in the nearby city of Lyons. While it is not clear what they discussed, it is clear that Pia, worried about Camus's poor health and impoverished circumstances, contacted Gallimard, the publisher of *The Stranger* and *The Myth of Sisyphus* (which Camus had dedicated to Pia). As a result, in late 1943 the renowned publishing house made Camus an offer he could not refuse: a job in Paris as a manuscript reader.

Shortly after Camus arrived in Paris, Pia made yet another offer to his former reporter that could not be refused: an editorial position on Combat's clandestine paper, also called *Combat*. Much of the work was logistical and practical—locating of paper and ink supplies, printing of copies, drafting other contributors—but all of the work carried real risks. In June 1944, when the Gestapo invaded the Lyons workshop that published *Combat*, the printer, André Bollier, took his own life after being wounded in a gun battle. One of Camus's closest colleagues, Jacqueline Bernard, was arrested and deported to the women's concentration camp of Ravensbruck. Perhaps closest to home, the friend Camus had recently made in Lyons, René Leynaud, was captured and executed by the Gestapo.

When not writing and rewriting his novel, Camus wrote columns for his paper. While none of the articles, for obvious reasons, carried bylines, Camus penned at least two and as many as four. Paradoxically, an article not definitively attributed to Camus—"You Will Be Judged by Your Actions"—is, at least to my ears, the most Camusian of the lot. Published just a month before the liberation of Paris, the article accuses Philippe Pétain not just of collaboration with Nazi Germany, but also of corruption of the French language. The latter, Camus warns, enabled the former. He declares Pétain to be "the supreme symbol of confusion," one whose regime called "patriots terrorists and murderers, bestowed the name 'honor' on what is simply resignation, 'order' on what is simply torture and 'loyalism' on what is simply murder." As Pétain's words had succeeded only in dividing and humiliating France, the sole antidote was "courage and plain speaking." We have reached a critical stage, Camus affirmed, "where every word counts and every word is a commitment."[42]

But it was in a series of four articles he wrote for other clandestine journals—later published as *Letters to a German Friend* and dedicated to Leynaud's memory—that Camus measured the long philosophical distance he traveled in the short time since his cycle of the absurd. In these missives to an imaginary German who has embraced the nihilism embodied by Hitler, Camus admits that the world is as silent now as it was for Meursault or, indeed, for himself. That the world remains mute, however, does not, or rather no longer means we must accept the world's meaningless. Neither a nihilistic nor a Nietzschean response will do. The Resistance had demonstrated with Cartesian clarity that when we join together to defend our dignity, we deposit meaning, if only ephemeral, in this shared effort on behalf of our shared humanity. "I know that the sky, which was indifferent to your appalling victories, will be equally indifferent to your just defeat. I expect nothing from it, even today." What Camus does expect, though, is that the act of resistance to Nazism "will have at least helped save man from the solitude you sought to send him."[43] How very similar to Rieux's laconic observation: "Since plague became in this way the duty of some men, it revealed itself as what it really was—the concern of all."[44]

In the novel's oft-quoted coda, Rieux reflects on the cries of joy rising from the city's residents when, the plague having lifted, so too does the quarantine. The doctor knows what the "jubilant did not know but could have learned from books: that the plague bacillus never dies or disappears for good." Ending his tale with the same image it began, he knows that one day the plague "would rouse up its rats again and send them forth to die in a happy city." A Sisyphus with a stethoscope, Rieux remembers what his city wishes to forget: that it is forever condemned to chronic convulsions of bacterial and ideological threats. Yet commentators, struck by this grimly stoic lesson, often overlook Rieux's earlier reflection following the death of Tarrou. He wonders what the friendship and the plague, now that both have ended, mean for him. Nothing more, nothing less that "all a man could win in the conflict between plague and life was knowledge and memories. But Tarrou, perhaps, would have called that winning the match."

And we, perhaps, can thus imagine both Rieux and ourselves happy.

EPILOGUE: FROM *THE LAST MAN* TO *THE FIRST MAN*

"We have strange news here," announces Lionel Verney, the narrator of Mary Shelley's *The Last Man*. Upon opening a London newspaper, he discovers that a disease that had devastated Constantinople is now spreading to Greece. Turning to a few friends, he wonders how they can best prevent the infection from reaching their shores. Scoffing, one friend replies: "It is as wise to discuss the probability of a visitation of the plague in our well-governed metropolis as to calculate the centuries which must escape before we can grow pineapples here in the open air."[1]

In an age of global warming, the sight of pineapple trees in Hyde Park would not be as strange as in 1824, when Shelley wrote these lines. Half a dozen years had passed since the publication of the novel for which the world now remembers her, *Frankenstein*, and nearly two years since the death of her husband, the poet Percy Bysshe Shelley, drowned when his boat was broken by a storm off the Italian coast. In 1823, the young widow had returned to England with her one surviving child—two others had died in infancy—after having spent five itinerant years on the continent.

A stranger in a newly strange country, Shelley found herself alone in England. Her friend Lord Byron was preparing for his fatal trip to Greece, while her father, the radical philosopher William Godwin, was utterly incapable of emotional and financial support. Nor could Shelley turn to her mother, the revolutionary feminist Mary Wollstonecraft, who had died upon giving birth to her daughter. It is hardly surprising that, shortly after her return to England, Shelley confided in her journal: "The Last Man! Yes, I may well describe that solitary being's feelings, feeling myself as the last relic of a beloved race, my companions extinct before me."[2]

Just as her experience of maternal abandonment infuses *Frankenstein*, Shelley's experience of social isolation and emotional desolation imbues *The Last Man*. Yet, while great upheavals of emotion mark both works, so too do great upheavals of thought. Skeptical about her age's exaltation of reason and idealization of nature, Shelley rejected her parents' revolutionary precepts and her husband's romantic ideals. Her doubts were strengthened by the writings of the conservative thinker Edmund Burke, particularly by his *Reflections on the Revolution in France*, where he had diagnosed the events on the other side of the Channel as a "plague." Soon enough, real pestilence burst onto the scene: in 1817, a number of Indian cities, most notably Bombay, were swept by cholera. British newspaper reports and parliamentary hearings, spurred by the country's vast commercial and economic stakes in India, captured the public's attention. While memories of the Great Plague had long receded, they were now replaced by fears of a new and equally virulent plague.

These fears were justified. Tragically, the great source of British wealth and prestige had now become its great scourge. Stowaways on British military and commercial ships, cholera bacilli had by the 1830s made their way from the Far and Middle East across the Baltic to Western Europe and North America. Though cholera was still a mostly local event in distant lands while she wrote her novel, Shelley proved prescient. Setting her novel in the year 2092—precisely three hundred years after the hatching of the revolutionary Terror in France—she anticipates not only the disease's global reach, but also the economic turmoil that would precede it. When thousands of miles still separate Great Britain from the plague, the country is nevertheless crippled by the evaporation of international trade. As the mysterious disease marches westward, its approach is announced by the collapse of commerce, closing of banks, scarcity of food, and mobbing of government offices by desperate citizens in search of relief. Indeed, Shelley makes clear the plague's principal means of transmission: the siege led by the hubristic Englishman Lord Raymond, of a plague-ridden Constantinople, let loose the plague on the rest of the world once the city's gates were forced open and its streets occupied by Raymond's soldiers.

Perhaps because it is the work of nature, not man, the plague's symptoms are not described in the same feverish detail as is Dr. Frankenstein's creation. The reader must read more than 250 pages of text before learning that the fatal disease's impact on the body is not all that hideous. It is certainly not as awful as cholera, which turns the digestive tract into a fire hose that empties the body, leaving behind a withered and black corpse. The symptoms of the disease in *The Last Man* are blurrier. It was unlike other diseases like typhus or smallpox, and Verney favors the ancient notion of miasma, or polluted air, that was still current in the early nineteenth century. When Verney sees a victim for the first time, we predictably learn more about this romantic's own feelings—"Cold were the sensations excited by words . . . compared to what I felt in looking at the corpse"—than the corpse's physical appearance.[3]

But while its signs are less horrid than cholera, the unnamed disease is far more severe. At the novel's end, the sole survivor—the last man—is Verney, who himself contracts, yet somehow recovers from, the disease. A case fatality rate of 100 percent from an infectious disease that spreads as widely and lasts as long—a biblical seven years—as does Shelley's is unthinkable. If a pathogen is too virulent, the historian William McNeill has observed, it will sign its own death warrant along with its host's. The reason has to do with laws of evolution: "Prolonged interaction between human host and infectious organism, carried on across many generations and among suitably numerous populations on each side, creates a pattern of mutual adaptation which allows both to survive."[4]

But it was precisely the unthinkable—another word, really, for the sublime—that Shelley wished to conjure. While England is still untouched by the plague, natural events herald its arrival. The climate turns volatile and violent, with great storms wreaking havoc with sea traffic and rupturing air traffic. The airships described by Shelley seem, at first glance, her one clear glimpse of the future, but she also foresees the catastrophic consequences of climate change. The combination of plague and storms lays waste to countries in the southern hemisphere, driving waves of refugees to Western Europe. "Many of the foreigners were utterly destitute," Verney observes, "and their increasing numbers at length forbade a recourse to the usual modes of relief."[5] The one difference that might strike a contemporary reader is that the government of the fictional England, rather than repelling the refugees, welcomes them, "affording aid to the victims of this calamity."[6] Soon enough, though, the collapse of global commerce and domestic markets means the government cannot aid its own, much less the mounting numbers of foreigners reaching England's shores.

The unprecedented and unworldly weather seems to reach a nearly biblical crescendo in the opening pages of the third and final volume. Like an Old Testament prophet, Verney demands to know if we hear "the rushing sound of the coming tempest" or "behold the clouds open, and destruction lurid and dire pour down on the blasted earth," all of which "announce the last days of man." Yet, it turns out not only is there no voice from the whirlwind, but the whirlwinds themselves abate. Rather than the Sturm und Drang we expect of an apocalypse conjured by a disenchanted romantic, it is instead heralded by an ambrosial and balmy spring, a radiant and flowering earth "rejoicing in the genial warmth of the unclouded empyrean."[7] With this unexpected turn, Shelley reveals not only that nature does quite well without a deity running the show, but also that nature does not give a particular hoot for the species that once believed it was running the show. As Verney sighs, "man, the queller of the elements, the lord of created nature, the peer of demi-gods, existed no longer."[8]

...

The plague Shelley conjures in her novel responds, in part, to her own desolate situation. Having not just lost all those individuals near to her, but also having lost faith in the ideals dear to them, Shelley sets the stage for the Judgment Day, though minus a divine judge, that will spell the end of humankind. What of the reign of reason heralded by her father and mother? It proves powerless to resist, much less cure the plague; it fails to prod leaders to acknowledge reality, much less act in a timely fashion to respond to it. Though they had ample warning, the English nevertheless refuse to believe the plague could reach their country, leaving Verney to sigh, "Fools that we were not long ago to have foreseen this."[9]

It turns out that reason is not just powerless to cure our passions, but it can become passion's slave. When the idealistic aristocrat Verney gives way to a shrewd populist named Ryland, he notes a paradox that has always bedeviled democracies. A public figure, Verney writes, who wishes "to do good who is patient, reasonable and gentle, yet disdains to use other argument than truth, has less influence over men's minds than he who, grasping and selfish, refuses not to adopt any means, nor awaken any passion, nor diffuse any falsehood, for the advancement of his cause. If this from time immemorial has been the case, the contrast was infinitely greater now that the one could bring harrowing fears and transcendent hopes into play."[10]

Not surprisingly, when the grasping and selfish Ryland learns that the plague has reached England, he thinks of his private, not the public good. His face twisted by fear, he tells Verney that everyone must flee. "The Plague. We must fly—all fly—but whither? No man can tell—there is no refuge on earth, it comes on us like a thousand packs of wolves—we must all fly." When Verney reminds him of his duties, Ryland explodes: "Duties! When I am a plague-spotted corpse, where will my duties be? Every man for himself!"[11] Following through on his panicky counsel, he flees into the countryside. Predictably, Verney discovers Ryland's body, half-eaten by insects, weeks later alone in a remote house.

A remote land is no safer from the disease than a remote house. In her earlier novel, *Frankenstein,* Shelley wraps up her tale in the vast and frozen expanses of the North Pole, where Victor Frankenstein, in fanatical pursuit of the creation that, exiled from his world, seeks to destroy it, comes to his end. *The Last Man* seems poised to end in the equally cold and forbidding landscape of the Alps. This is where Verney and Adrian, leading a "train half dead" of followers, fly in the hope of escaping the plague. The hope turns out to be as vain and teasing as the setting is bleak and fitting. "Sublime grandeur of outward objects soothed our hapless hearts and were in harmony with our desolation," Verney marvels. "Our misery took its majestic shape and colouring from the vast ruin, that accompanied and made one with it."[12]

In this case, misery does not love company: the feeble few who reach the Alps die there. Having carried off everyone but Verney, Adrian, and their young charge Clara, the plague dies then as well. But Verney soon loses his two remaining companions who, like Shelley, drown during a storm in the Adriatic. Seemingly alone in the world, Verney is left to grasp for meaning. When he was still in the Alps, the thought of the saving powers of art and love stopped him from leaping off the nearest precipice. Nevertheless, he cannot help but ask himself, "Did God create man, merely in the end to become dead earth in the midst of healthful, vegetating nature? Was he of no more account to his Maker, than a field of corn blighted in the ear? Were our proud dreams thus to fade?"[13]

Yet this conviction, already bending under the weight of plague, seems to break when Verney is the last man standing, with no one to love and, perhaps, no reason to create. When the plague had first made landfall in England, Verney held back from ending his life thanks to the "powers of love, poetry and creative fancy that will dwell even beside the sick of the plague, with the squalid, and with the dying."[14] By the novel's end, though, both art and love disappear as the plague disappears and no one is left to die. As he wanders the streets of Rome, surrounded by "truncated columns, broken capitals . . . which once made part of the palace of the Caesars," Verney resembles the ancient traveler in Percy Shelley's "Ozymandias," who spies in a vast desert a statue's shattered remains near a now-empty pedestal engraved with the words: "My name is Ozymandias, King of Kings; look on my Works, ye Mighty, and despair!" As for the statues still standing intact, they instill Verney with a different kind of despair. "Often, half in bitter mockery, and half in self-delusion, I clasped their icy proportions, and, coming between Cupid and his Psyche's lips, pressed the unconceiving marble."[15]

...

No less unconceiving is the sky over the Algeria of Albert Camus. It is not surprising that a Shelley scholar, Anne Mellor, draws a straight line from the pessimism of Shelley to the absurdism of Camus. For both writers, Mellor writes, "all meaning resides, not in an indifferent universe, but in human relationships and language-systems which are inherently temporal and doomed to end."[16]

What Mellor misses, however, is that while the sky remains indifferent and human relationships are doomed to end, we are not doomed to meaningless lives. The same landscape and skyscape that resisted meaning in Camus's earlier novels, *The Stranger* and *The Plague*, are transformed in his last and incomplete work, *The First Man*. In 1947, when *The Plague* was published, Camus was already looking ahead, taking notes for a new series of works, one he baptized the cycle of love. He began drafting the novel as part of the cycle, but did not live to complete it. In January 1960, when Camus was killed in a car accident, the unfinished manuscript of 144 handwritten pages was found near his body. It was more than three decades later, in 1994, that the manuscript, titled *Le premier homme*, or *The First Man*, was published to international acclaim.

The unfinished novel is about an unfinished life. Traveling to a military cemetery, the protagonist Jacques Cormery finds the grave of his father, killed at the Battle of the Marne when his son was still an infant. Staring at the dates on the gravestone, 1885–1914, the forty-year-old Cormery realizes with a start that he is now older than the twenty-nine-year-old Henri Cormery had been when a bullet pierced his skull. Indeed, apart from the way his father died, Cormery knows as little about him as he does about his deaf and mostly silent mother. While it is not a mystery that Cormery and Camus are mostly one and the same, the novel's beginning points to the inevitable mystery to each of our lives: who am I and how did I come to be so. This, I think, explains the entry in Camus's journal describing the novel as a "journey in order to discover his secret: he is not the first. Every man is the first man, nobody is."

His memory stirred by a grave marker, not a madeleine, Cormery undertakes his own *recherche du temps perdu*, a personal archaeology that drives him to dig into the past and find the people who had shaped his life and character. "No one ever talked about them. Neither his mother nor his uncle ever spoke of the departed relatives. Nor of the father whose traces he was seeking, nor of the others."[17] Dominating this landscape of the dead and forgotten is Cormery's mother. He recalls when, still a child, he would return home to their bare apartment and see his mother sitting by the window, staring silently at the street and the people and cars she could not hear. "The child would stop on the doorsill, his heart heavy, full of despairing love for his mother, and for something in his mother that did not belong or no longer belonged to the world and to the triviality of the days."[18]

Even as an adult, Camus, like Cormery, struggled to find the words for this "something." Though he was so closely tied to the sensual and physical world, Camus seems to be trying to capture something outside this world. Is it possible that this "something"—this quality that escapes our mundane lives—has a reality independent of the world we inhabit, but at the same time informs it? At the University of Algiers, Camus wrote his dissertation on Saint Augustine—whom he called "the other North African"—and the Hellenistic philosopher Plotinus. The metaphysics of Plato deeply influenced these thinkers, both of whom viewed the world as a place of appearances where we live our lives of exile from another and greater reality. The young Camus argued, however, that while Plotinus agreed with Augustine that life in this world was shadow play, he differed in his insistence on the role of art in bridging the two worlds. For Plotinus, he wrote, "philosophy is not merely a religious mode of thinking but an artist's way of looking at things as well."[19]

While this mode of thinking is absent from Camus's earlier cycles, I have the impression he turns to it as he begins his third cycle. Not long before his death, Camus wrote that his literary ambition was to recount "the admirable silence of a mother and one man's effort to rediscover a justice or a love to match this silence." By justice, I think Camus meant *doing* justice: to recognize and render the enduring truth of a particular moment, the abiding essence to a particular life. This is a supremely demanding task. What Iris Murdoch wrote of love applies to art: "it is the extremely difficult realization that something other than oneself is real."[20] Camus keeps reminding himself of this task in what would be among his last notebook jottings. In a 1958 entry, titled "Stages of Healing," Camus includes: "Remain close to the reality of beings and things. Return as often as possible to personal happiness. Not refusing to recognize what is true even when the truth happens to thwart the desirable."[21] During a trip to Greece that same year, he adds: "Live in and for the truth. The truth of what we are foremost. Quit compromising with people. The truth of what is. Don't be tricky with reality."[22] After returning to France, Camus holds fast to his experience in Greece: "The lie lulls or dreams, like illusion. The truth is the only power, cheerful, inexhaustible. If we were able to live only of, and for truth: young and immortal energy in us. The man of truth does not age. A little more effort, and he will not die."[23]

During a visit to Algiers, Cormery regards his mother sitting by the window, "isolated by her semi-deafness, her difficulty in expressing herself, beautiful surely but virtually inaccessible, and never more so than when she was full of smiles and when his own heart most went out to her."[24] Yes, of course, don't be tricky with reality. But what to do when a particular reality is so very elusive? Camus keeps circling the image of his mother, trying to convey, through art, the "something" that she embodied. We glimpse this in *The Plague*, when Rieux returns home to find his mother, like the mothers of both Camus and Cormery, gazing tranquilly and silently out of the window in the dining room. When Rieux excuses himself from always being away from home, his mother replies: "I don't mind waiting, if I know you're going to come back. And when you aren't here, I think of what you are doing."[25] In other words, Rieux is never not there to his mother. And, despite her silence, she is never not there for him.

Looking back on his two earlier cycles, Camus understood they did not fully explain or encompass the human situation. He had advanced from absurdity to rebellion, but rebellion in turn was impossible to maintain without knowing a "kind of love that remains to be defined."[26] He never fully defined it during his short life; he would never have fully defined it had he lived longer. No one ever has. But Camus knew that, like his mother, while love seemed remote, it was nevertheless always already there. Shortly before his death, he wrote that his mother's love, though silent, “has never ceased speaking to me.” Without its silent yet abiding presence, this particular first man would have been the last man. Absurdity is king, Camus once remarked, “but love saves us from it.”[27] While we would be foolish to hope this is always true, we should never despair that it might be.

...

While I was revising this manuscript, I received a call from J., the physical therapist known as Blessed Abundance to some of the nursing home residents. Several months have passed since I last set foot in the home, but J. always sends me news of the residents. She tells me about the exchanges she has had and glimpses she has caught of those men and women I had gotten to know at the home. There have been no deaths this year, but too many died and died alone last year, all of them due to COVID-related causes. J. told me the administration would hold a memorial service and, by way of commemorating those lives, plant seventeen Texas rosebushes in the courtyard where I would sit with Mr. R and Mrs. W. Suddenly, I remembered standing with J. while Mrs. R sang her songs of Texas, punctuated by her wispy yodels. “I love y’all, darlings. Give me a kiss.” We pointed dumbly, helplessly, to our KN95 masks.

But J. had called for another reason as well. Moments earlier, she had passed by the residence’s bistro—the optimistic name given to the drab dining hall shut since March 2020—and stopped in disbelief. The bistro was back in business, she told me. At each of the fifteen or so tables sat a single resident, some brought in on wheelchairs and others who brought themselves on walkers. While the nurses’ aides delivered the food trays to the tables, the residents waved to one another across the room. Many of them were newly coiffed for the occasion—the previous week J. mentioned that the hair stylist, to great cheer, had also reopened—and their hair glowed as brightly as their smiles.

Her voice thickening a bit, J. told me that she then glimpsed one of her favorite residents, Mrs. M, sitting at the piano. One of my favorites as well, Mrs. M was a retired music teacher in her early eighties. Though confined to a wheelchair, she was always in movement, propelling herself along the hallways. Whenever she zipped past me, bent over as much by sheer determination as by her degenerative scoliosis, I had the distinct impression that the bright red scarf always knotted around her neck was flapping wildly in her wind stream. When I brought her meal trays, Mrs. M would often beam and gesture to me with her hand to come closer. She had a story to tell, but her voice—due to a botched operation on her vocal cords—had become fudged and faint. Taking a chair beside her, I would lean over and listen to one of her many tales as a teacher, of the recitals she staged, the students she loved, the music they played. What Mrs. M did not tell me, but I had learned from J., were the stories of abuse she had endured from her husband, whom she eventually left with her two small children in tow. Now adults, her children were very close to their mother and, like Mrs. M, rubbed raw by the imposed separation.

But now, the separations were drawing to an end. Not only were Mrs. M's children again visiting, but her fellow residents were again gathering together. No less important, she was again providing the soundtrack to their meals. Leaning over while arranging her sheet music, Mrs. M must have felt J.'s eyes on her. She turned in her direction, flashed a brilliant smile and, turning back to the keyboard, launched into a rendition of "Beauty and the Beast." J. told me that Mrs. M played it without fault and, upon reaching the end, the room bubbled with applause. As for J., she hurried away and burst into tears.

Since the phone call with J., I cannot help but think about the moment she experienced. I also started to cry when J. told me her story. Pure kitsch, I keep telling myself. Yet I also keep telling myself that kitsch is not only not necessarily bad, but at times as good as it gets, even or especially when we recognize it as kitsch. In his novel *The Unbearable Lightness of Being*, which is something of an extended meditation on kitsch, Milan Kundera insists that kitsch is the "folding screen set up to curtain off death." But he also suggests that when we see kitsch for what it is, it becomes as moving as any other human frailty. "No matter how we scorn it," this great ironist concedes, "kitsch is an integral part of the human condition." J.'s tears, my tears, no doubt the tears of others in the room, remind us of our common condition as frail and flawed human beings. For that matter, those tears—as much for us as for others, for those we lost during the pandemic and what we ourselves will one day lose—remind each of us that we are all of us both the last and first of women and men.

ACKNOWLEDGMENTS

I wish to thank Alan Thomas, my editor at the University of Chicago Press, for his calm guidance, sharp intelligence, and great decency. I would not have written this book were it not for him. My thanks, as well, to his team at Chicago, who never lost their patience with my bouts of tardiness and impatience. A superb poet, Carrie Olivia Adams, has also been a superb (and patient) marketing director. My copyeditor, Marianne Tatom, has been no less superb; her sharp eye has saved me from several embarrassments.

I must also thank David Phillips, the chair of the Philosophy Department at the University of Houston, who kindly allowed me to teach a course on writers and plagues in spring 2021. No less important, I am deeply grateful to my students in that class, in particular Michael Kurian, Lena Craven, Oulu Li, Sarah Philip, Robert Gomez, and Vero Poppe for their insights and questions. My sincere thanks, as well, to George Alliger, Michael Barnes, Laura Secor, Joel Weickgenant, and Lois Zamora for their support and suggestions.

Finally, I need to thank J., the physical therapist at the nursing home where I volunteered in 2020 and first had the idea for this book. As I note in the book, some of the residents called her Blessed Abundance. Though I am not religious, I cannot think of a better name for this remarkable person. I will never forget the impact that her unwavering kindness and attention had upon those who came into her life at the residence.

This book is dedicated to the residents themselves. Though I cannot name them or their residence, I have done my best in this book to show why I will never forget them.

NOTES

INTRODUCTION

1 https://www.theguardian.com/science/2016/feb/28/loneliness-is-like-an-iceberg-john-cacioppo-social-neuroscience-interview.

2 Nicholas Christakis, *Apollo's Arrow: The Profound and Enduring Impact of Coronavirus on the Way We Live* (New York: Little, Brown Spark, 2020), 15.

3 Iris Murdoch, *Existentialists and Mystics: Writings on Philosophy and Literature*, ed. Peter Conradi (New York: Penguin, 1997), 294.

CHAPTER ONE

1 https://www.the-tls.co.uk/articles/the-first-pandemic-in-western-literature/.

2 As Michael MacKinnon notes, there are archaeological finds that reveal the presence of black rats in ancient Greece. *The Oxford Handbook of Animals in Classical Thought and Life*, ed. Gordon Campbell (Oxford 2014), 173.

3 https://www.academia.dk/BiologiskAntropologi/PDF/Paleomicrobiology/10.pdf.

4 Richard Schlatter, "Thomas Hobbes and Thucydides," *Journal of the History of Ideas* 6 (1945): 357.

5 Gregory Crane, *Thucydides and the Ancient Simplicity: The Limits of Political Realism* (Berkeley: University of California Press, 1998), 285.

6 *Twilight of the Idols*, trans. Richard Hollingdale (New York: Penguin, 1990), 118.

7 W. Robert Connor, *Thucydides* (Princeton, NJ: Princeton University Press, 1984), 5.

8 Connor, *Thucydides*, 247.

9 Garry Wills, *Lincoln at Gettysburg: The Words That Remade America* (New York: Simon & Schuster, 1992), 41. The Hellenist Nicole Loraux surveys the many

ways in which Pericles's oration was used and abused over the centuries. See her book *The Invention of Athens: The Funeral Oration in the Classical City*, trans. Alan Sheridan (Cambridge, MA: Harvard University Press, 1986).

10 In his translation of the book of Job, the biblical scholar Robert Alter places the author in either the late sixth or fifth century BCE. See his *The Wisdom Books* (New York: Norton, 2010), 5.

11 https://ge.usembassy.gov/remarks-by-president-trump-and-members-of-the-coronavirus-task-force-in-press-briefing-april-18/.

12 Herodotus, *The History*, trans. David Greene (Chicago: University of Chicago Press, 1987), 59.

13 Michael Scott, *Delphi: A History of the Center of the Ancient World* (Princeton, NJ: Princeton University Press, 2014), 15.

14 Hugh Bowden, *Classical Athens and the Delphic Oracle: Divination and Democracy* (Cambridge: Cambridge University Press, 2005), 73.

15 Bowden, *Classical Athens and the Delphic Oracle*, 75.

16 Victor Davis Hanson, *A War Like No Other* (New York: Random House, 2005), 81.

CHAPTER TWO

1 Susan Mattern, *The Prince of Medicine: Galen in the Roman Empire* (New York: Oxford University Press, 2013), 24–25.

2 Mattern, *The Prince of Medicine*, 126.

3 Kyle Harper, *The Fate of Rome* (Princeton, NJ: Princeton University Press, 2017), 99.

4 Anthony Birley, *Marcus Aurelius* (New Haven, CT: Yale University Press, 1966), 116.

5 Marguerite Yourcenar, *Memoirs of Hadrian*, trans. Grace Frick and Marguerite Yourcenar (New York: FSG, 1963), 269.

6 All citations are from Marcus Aurelius, *Meditations*, trans. Martin Hammond (London: Penguin, 2006).

7 Mattern, *The Prince of Medicine*, 188.

8 Mattern, *The Prince of Medicine*, 197.

9 Pierre Hadot, *La citadelle intérieure: Introduction aux Pensées de Marc Aurèle* (Paris: Fayard, 1992), 155.

10 Quoted in *Companion to Marcus Aurelius*, ed. Marcel Van Ackeren (London: Wiley-Blackwell, 2012), 454.

11 Hadot, *La citadelle intérieure*, 65.

12 Harper, *The Fate of Rome*, 68.

13 Mattern, *The Prince of Medicine*, 203.

14 Harper, *The Fate of Rome*, 101.

15 Birley, *Marcus Aurelius*, 150.

16 Birley, *Marcus Aurelius*, 160.

17 See Christer Bruun, "The Antonine Plague and the 'Third-Century Crisis,'" in *Crises and the Roman Empire*, ed. Olivier Hekster (Leiden: Brill, 2007).

18 Bruce Frier, "Demography," in the *Cambridge Ancient History*, ed. Alan Bowman (Cambridge: Cambridge University Press, 1982), 816.

19 Harper, *The Fate of Rome*, 115.

20 Martha Nussbaum, *The Therapy of Desire: Theory and Practice in Hellenistic Ethics* (Princeton, NJ: Princeton University Press, 1994), 345.

21 Michel Foucault, *Corps écrit*, no. 5 (February 1983): 3–23.

22 Quoted in Nussbaum, *The Therapy of Desire*, 330.

23 Martin Beckmann, *The Column of Marcus Aurelius: The Genesis and Meaning of the Roman Imperial Monument* (Chapel Hill: University of North Carolina Presss, 2011), 196.

24 Cassius Dio, *Roman History*, Loeb Classical Library (1927), section 16, https://penelope.uchicago.edu/Thayer/E/Roman/Texts/Cassius_Dio/72*.html.

25 Quoted in Nussbaum, *The Therapy of Desire*, 400.

CHAPTER THREE

1 Philippe Desan, *Montaigne: A Life*, trans. Steven Rendall and Lisa Neal (Princeton, NJ: Princeton University Press, 2018), 471.

2 Quoted in Laurent Coste, "Bordeaux et le peste dans la première moitié du XVIIème siècle," in *Annales du Midi* (1998), 457.

3 One contemporary, Joseph Scaliger, estimated that 16,000 had died, while the chronicler Gabriel de Lurbe believed the number of deaths to be 14,000. See *Lettres françaises inédites de Joseph Scaliger*, ed. Philippe de Larroque (Paris: Picard, 1879), 202.

4 Donald Frame, *Montaigne: A Biography* (San Francisco: North Point Press, 1984), 240.

5 *The Complete Works of Montaigne*, trans. Donald Frame (Stanford, CA: Stanford University Press, 1965), 1328–1329.

6 Michel Signoli and Stéfan Tzortzis, "La Peste à Marseilles et dans le sud-est de la France en 1720–1722," *Cahiers de la Méditerranée* 96 (2018): 217.

7 Jean-Baptiste Bertand, *Relation historique de la peste de Marseille en 1720* (Cologne: Pierre Marteau, 1721), 6–7.

8 Emmanuel LeRoy Ladurie, "Motionless History," *Social Science History* 1, no. 2 (Winter 1977): 124.

9 "Of Practice," in *The Complete Essays of Montaigne*, trans. Donald Frame (Palo Alto, CA: Stanford University Press, 1965), 272.

10 *The Discourse of Voluntary Servitude*, trans. Harry Kurz (Indianapolis: Liberty Fund, 1942), 2.

11 "Of Friendship," in *Essays*, 144.

12 "Of Friendship," in *Essays*, 139.

13 *The Hour of Our Death*, trans. Helen Weaver (New York: Knopf, 1981), 5–29.

14 "Letter to His Father," in *The Complete Works of Michel de Montaigne*, trans. Donald Frame (New York: Knopf, 2003), 1284.

15 "Letter to His Father," 1288.

16 "Of Physiognomy," in *Essays*, 801.

17 "Of Physiognomy," in *Essays*, 802.

18 "Of Physiognomy," in *Essays*, 66.

19 "Of Idleness," in *Essays*, 21.

20 "Of the Affection of Fathers," in *Essays*, 278.

21 "Three Kinds of Association," in *Essays*, 629.

22 "Of Repentance," in *Essays*, 611.

23 "Of Experiences," in *Essays*, 821.

24 "That the Taste of Good and Evil Depends in Large Part on the Opinion We Have of Them," in *Essays*, 46.

25 "That to Philosophize Is to Learn How to Die," in *Essays*, 60.

26 "That to Philosophize Is to Learn How to Die," in *Essays*, 57. This sentiment smacks of Hamlet, and it may well be because Shakespeare had read the freshly translated essays by his acquaintance John Florio while writing the play. After all, the Prince of Denmark spends his short life essaying the significance of death. As he tells Horatio shortly before his duel with Laertes, "If it be now, 'tis not to come; if it be not to come, it will be now; if it be not now, yet it will come—the readiness is all." It's not the ghost of his father, but of Montaigne, that haunts Hamlet when he utters this line.

27 Mack P. Holt, *The French Wars of Religion, 1562–1629* (Cambridge: Cambridge University Press, 1995), 60.

28 "Of Physiognomy," in *Essays*, 800.

29 Holt, *The French Wars of Religion*, 86–87.

30 Desan, *Montaigne*, 230–231.

31 For an excellent account, see Martha Nussbaum, *The Therapy of Desire: Theory and Practice in Hellenistic Ethics* (Princeton, NJ: Princeton University Press, 1994), 280–315.

32 "An Apology for Raymond Sebond," in *Essays*, 374.

33 "An Apology for Raymond Sebond," in *Essays*, 374.

34 "Of Freedom of Conscience," in *Essays*, 506.

35 "Of Custom," in *Essays*, 86.

36 "Of Cannibals," in *Essays*, 157.

37 Alexander Nehamas, *The Art of Living: Socratic Reflections from Plato to Foucault* (Berkeley: University of California Press, 1998), 44.

38 Stefan Zweig, *Montaigne*, French trans. J.-J. Lafaye and François Brugier (Paris: PUF, 1981), 118.

39 George Prochnik, *The Impossible Exile: Stefan Zweig at the End of the World* (Boston: Other Press, 2014), 336.

40 Prochnik, *The Impossible Exile*, 3.

41 Prochnik, *The Impossible Exile*, 3.

42 Zweig, *Montaigne*, 13–14.
43 Zweig, *Montaigne*, 118–120.
44 "Of Physiognomy," in *Essays*, 796.
45 "Of Experience," in *Essays*, 854.
46 "Of Experience," in *Essays*, 804–805.
47 "Of Experience," in *Essays*, 852.
48 "Of Experience," in *Essays*, 852.
49 "Of Experience," in *Essays*, 857.
50 "Of Experience," in *Essays*, 830.

CHAPTER FOUR

1 Michel Signoli and Stéfan Tzortzis, "La peste à Marseille et dans le sud-est de la France en 1720–1722: les épidémies d'Orient de retour en Europe," in *Cahiers de la Méditerranée* 96 (2018): 220.
2 Quoted in Daniel Gordon, "The City and the Plague in the Age of Enlightenment," in *Yale French Studies* 92 (1997): 83.
3 Gordon, "The City and the Plague in the Age of Enlightenment," 85.
4 Signoli and Tzortis, "La peste à Marseille," 224.
5 Quoted in M.E. Novak, "Defoe and the Disordered City," *PMLA* 92, no. 2 (1989): 245.
6 https://thehistoryofparliament.wordpress.com/2020/04/09/where-the-disease-is-desperate-the-remedy-must-be-so-too-debating-the-1721-quarantine-act/.
7 Paula Backsheider, *Daniel Defoe: His Life* (Baltimore: Johns Hopkins Press, 1989), 426.
8 Backsheider, *Daniel Defoe*, 504.
9 William Lee, *Daniel Defoe: His Life and Recently Discovered Writings*, vol. 2 (London: Camden, 1869), 379.
10 Lee, *Daniel Defoe*, vol. 2, 379.
11 https://www.houstonchronicle.com/news/investigations/article/How-many-missed-Texas-is-second-worst-in-the-15193258.php.
12 Niall Boyce, "Bills of Mortality: Tracking Disease in Early-Modern London," *The Lancet* 395 (April 11, 2020): 1186.
13 Nicholas Seager, "Lies, Damned Lies and Statistics: Epistemology and Fiction in Defoe's Journal of the Plague Year," *Modern Language Review* 103, no. 3 (July 2008): 243–244.
14 Daniel Defoe, *Due Preparations for the Plague, as well for Soul as Body* (London, 1722), 108.
15 Defoe, *Due Preparations for the Plague*, 197.
16 Defoe, *Due Preparations for the Plague*, 4.
17 Defoe, *Due Preparations for the Plague*, 7–8.
18 Defoe, *Due Preparations for the Plague*, 9.

19 Defoe, *Due Preparations for the Plague*, 18.
20 Defoe, *Due Preparations for the Plague*, 43.
21 William H. McNeill, *Plagues and Peoples* (New York: Random House, 1998), 181.
22 Daniel Defoe, *A Journal of the Plague Year* (New York: Penguin, 2013), 48.
23 Defoe, *Journal*, 152.
24 Defoe, *Journal*, 160.
25 Defoe, *Journal*, 12.
26 Quoted in John Richetti, *The Life of Daniel Defoe: A Critical Biography* (London: Wiley, 2005), 239.
27 Defoe, *Journal*, 74.
28 Defoe, *Journal*, 184.
29 Defoe, *Journal*, 78–79.
30 Defoe, *Journal*, 60–61.
31 Inge Clendinnen, *Reading the Holocaust* (New York: Cambridge University Press, 1999), 183.
32 Defoe, *Journal*, 99.
33 Defoe, *Journal*, 116.
34 Defoe, *Journal*, 102ff.
35 Defoe, *Journal*, 31.
36 Defoe, *Journal*, 109.
37 Defoe, *Journal*, 34.
38 Catherine Rubincam, "Thucydides and Defoe: Two Plague Narratives," *International Journal of the Classical Tradition* 11 (Fall 2004): 194–212.
39 Defoe, *Journal*, 35.
40 Maximillian Novak, *Daniel Defoe, Master of Fictions: His Life and Ideas* (New York: Oxford University Press, 2001), 158.
41 Defoe, *Journal*, 111.
42 Defoe, *Journal*, 27.
43 Defoe, *Journal*, 225.

CHAPTER FIVE

1 Albert Camus, *The Myth of Sisyphus*, trans. Justin O'Brien (New York: Random House, 1958), 3.
2 Camus, *The Myth of Sisyphus*, 21.
3 Camus, *The Myth of Sisyphus*, 6.
4 Camus, *The Myth of Sisyphus*, 53.
5 Albert Camus, "The Minotaur, Or Stopping in Oran," in *Lyrical and Critical Essays*, trans. Ellen Conroy Kennedy (New York: Random Books, 1970), 112, 113, 118.
6 *Albert Camus & Jean Grenier: Correspondence, 1932–1960*, trans. Jan Rigaud (Lincoln: University of Nebraska Press, 2003), 43.

7 Albert Camus, *Oeuvres completes (OC)*, t. 2, ed. Jacqueline Lévi-Valensi (Paris: Gallimard, 2006), 259.

8 *Carnets, Janvier 1942–mars 1951* (Paris: Gallimard, 1964), 36. Italics in original.

9 Albert Camus, *The Plague*, trans. Stuart Gilbert (New York: Random House, 1991), 7.

10 Camus, *The Plague*, 17.

11 Camus, *OC*, 273.

12 Adrien Proust, *La Défense de l'Europe contre la peste* (Paris: Masson et Cie, 1897), 5.

13 Mika McKinnon, "Are Rats Innocent of Spreading the Black Plague?," *Smithsonian Magazine* (January 17, 2018), https://www.smithsonianmag.com/smart-news/are-rats-innocent-spreading-black-plague-180967855/.

14 Hans Zinsser, *Rats, Lice and History* (London: Routledge, 1935), 191.

15 *Carnets*, 50.

16 Camus made this point in his famous exchange with the literary critic Roland Barthes in 1955. See the reproduction of this exchange in Jacqueline Lévi-Valensi, *La Peste d'Albert Camus* (Paris: Gallimard, 1991), 183–193.

17 Lévi-Valensi, *La Peste d'Albert Camus*, 72.

18 Camus, *The Plague*, 301.

19 Camus, *The Plague*, 12.

20 Albert Camus, *Notebooks: 1951–1959*, trans. Ryan Bloom (New York: Ivan Dee, 2008), 70.

21 George Orwell, "A Hanging," in *The Orwell Reader* (New York: Harcourt Brace Jovanovich, 1956), 11.

22 Iris Murdoch, *The Sovereignty of Good* (New York: Routledge & Kegan Paul, 2007), 89. Italics in original.

23 Quoted in Marianne Ruel Robins, "The Grey Site of Memory: Le Chambon-sur-Lignon and Protestant Exceptionalism on the Plateau Vivarais-Lignon," *Church History* (June 2013): 317.

24 Philip Hallie, *Lest Innocent Blood Be Shed: The Story of Le Chambon and How Goodness Happened There* (New York: Harper & Row, 1979).

25 See *Le Plateau Vivrais-Lignon: Actes du colloque du Chambon-sur-Lignon*, ed. Pierre Bolle (Le Chambon: Société de l'histoire du Montagne, 1992), as well as Robins's richly documented article.

26 Robins, "The Grey Site of Memory," 330.

27 Robins, "The Grey Site of Memory," 329.

28 Robins, "The Grey Site of Memory," 352.

29 See Sauvage's remarkable film *Weapons of the Spirit*.

30 Robins, "The Grey Site of Memory," 339.

31 Murdoch, *The Sovereignty of Good*, 55.

32 Camus, *Notebooks*, 69.

33 Herbert Lottman, *Albert Camus: A Biography* (Corte Madera, CA: Gingko Press, 1997), 289.

34 Olivier Todd, *Albert Camus, Une Vie* (Paris: Gallimard, 1996), 321.

35 Camus, *Notebooks*, 55.

36 Camus, *Notebooks*, 60. Italics in original.

37 Camus, *Notebooks*, 42.

38 "De l'insignificance," in *Oeuvres complètes*, t. 3, ed. Raymond Gay-Croisier (Paris: Gallimard, 2008), 389.

39 "Against Dryness," in *Existentialists and Mystics: Writings on Philosophy and Literature*, ed. Peter Conradi (New York: Penguin, 1997), 294.

40 Murdoch, *The Sovereignty of Good*, 36.

41 Camus, *Notebooks*, 165.

42 *Camus at Combat: Writing 1944–1947*, trans. Arthur Goldhammer (Princeton, NJ: Princeton University Press, 2006), 8.

43 Albert Camus, *Lettres à un ami allemand* (Paris: Gallimard, 1948), 78.

44 Camus, *The Plague*, 132 (with my changes).

EPILOGUE

1 Mary Shelley, *The Last Man* (Oxford: Oxford University Press, 1994), 220–221.

2 Quoted in Morton D. Paley, "The Last Man: Apocalypse without Millennium," in *The Other Mary Shelley: Beyond Frankenstein*, ed. Audrey Fisch (Oxford: Oxford University Press, 1993), 109.

3 Shelley, *The Last Man*, 259.

4 William H. McNeill, *Plagues and Peoples* (New York: Random House, 1998), 27–28.

5 Shelley, *The Last Man*, 232–233.

6 Shelley, *The Last Man*, 236.

7 Shelley, *The Last Man*, 315.

8 Shelley, *The Last Man*, 320.

9 Shelley, *The Last Man*, 248.

10 Shelley, *The Last Man*, 386.

11 Shelley, *The Last Man*, 242.

12 Shelley, *The Last Man*, 424.

13 Shelley, *The Last Man*, 398.

14 Shelley, *The Last Man*, 275.

15 Shelley, *The Last Man*, 465.

16 Anne Mellor, *Mary Shelley: Her Life, Her Fiction, Her Monsters* (London: Routledge, 1989), 169.

17 Albert Camus, *The First Man*, trans. David Hapgood (New York: Knopf, 1995), 133.

18 Camus, *The First Man*, 171.

19 *Christian Metaphysics and Neo-Platonism*, trans. Joseph McBride (New York: St Martin's Press, 1992), 126.

20 Iris Murdoch, "The Sublime and the Good," in *Existentialists and Mystics*, ed. Peter Conradi (New York: Penguin, 1997), 215.

21 Albert Camus, *Notebooks: 1951–1959*, trans. Ryan Bloom (New York: Ivan Dee, 2008), 204.

22 Camus, *Notebooks*, 215.

23 Camus, *Notebooks*, 216.

24 Camus, *The Last Man*, 58.

25 Albert Camus, *The Plague*, trans. Stuart Gilbert (New York: Random House, 1991), 123.

26 Albert Camus, *Oeuvres complètes*, t. 2 (Paris: Gallimard, 2006), 1068.

27 Camus, *Notebooks*, 93.

INDEX